FINANCIAL PSYCHEDELIA
AND THE COMMONS

FINANCIAL PSYCHEDELIA
AND THE COMMONS

Andrea Fumagalli

BLOOMSBURY ACADEMIC

LONDON • NEW YORK • OXFORD • NEW DELHI • SYDNEY

BLOOMSBURY ACADEMIC
Bloomsbury Publishing Plc, 50 Bedford Square, London, WC1B 3DP, UK
Bloomsbury Publishing Inc, 1359 Broadway, New York, NY 10018, USA
Bloomsbury Publishing Ireland, 29 Earlsfort Terrace, Dublin 2, D02 AY28, Ireland

BLOOMSBURY, BLOOMSBURY ACADEMIC and the Diana logo are trademarks
of Bloomsbury Publishing Plc

First published in Great Britain 2026

A catalogue record for this book is available from the British Library.

Library of Congress Cataloging-in-Publication Data available

ISBN: HB: 978-1-3504-1385-6
PB: 978-1-3504-1384-9
ePDF: 978-1-3504-1387-0
eBook: 978-1-3504-1386-3

Series: In Common

Typeset by Newgen KnowledgeWorks Pvt. Ltd., Chennai, India
Printed and bound in Great Britain

For product safety related questions contact productsafety@bloomsbury.com.

To find out more about our authors and books visit www.bloomsbury.com
and sign up for our newsletters.

CONTENTS

ACKNOWLEDGEMENTS

It was about the beginning of February 1972, if I remember correctly. I was soon to turn thirteen. A friend with whom I played tennis, Giovanni Musio, gave me a double record, saying: 'My older brother gave it to me. It's strange music, not really rock or beat. I don't like it, if you want to take it. You should like it.' About a couple of months earlier, wandering as I did every Saturday on my way home from school among the stalls of the Senigallia fair in Milan, which was taking place right under the windows of my house, a long-haired man (a character I was both terrified of and attracted to), at the corner of Via Calatafini and Via San Luca in Milano, stopped me and said: 'Listen to this record. It's a bomb!' 'But I have no money, only 100 lire.' 'Alright, give me those.' I went home and after lunch, locked in my room, making sure nobody came in, almost as if I were smoking a joint, I put that vinyl on the platter. It was The Doors' first record. Two tracks blew me away: 'Light My Fire' and 'The End' – not to mention 'Break on Through (To the Other Side)'. Another band, other than the Beatles and the Rolling Stones! I began to get interested in the kind of music they called acid rock or psychedelic rock and to talk about it with friends. I was then very interested when Giovanni Musio gave me that record a few months later. So interested that, after listening to it the first time, I listened to it several more times. It was the double live album, *Live/ Dead*, by the Grateful Dead.

Without that gift, this book would never have been written. And without the hippy dealers of good music at the Senigallia fair, on the corner of Via Calatafini and Via San Luca, sitting on the ground, with their boxes of records, I might not have fallen in love and remained addicted to psychedelic music.

To Giovanni Musio (with whom I have lost touch) and the hippies of the Senigallia fair, my first thanks and dedication.

In the course of my life, especially during the 1970s, I was able to delve into the themes and reasons behind rock music. This interest was also a kind of political initiation. Radical transformations in society are often accompanied by new styles of music. Rock music was this and this was its social value, like other musical expressions: moments of political identification and intersubjective communication, necessary conditions for initiating a political process. I therefore have rock music to thank for the fact that I began to take an interest in politics, as early as the 1970s, during high school. To think that back then, lying in bed, you could choose whether to listen to Jimi Hendrix or Pink Floyd or King Crimson, Moby Grape or The Jeffersons or Quicksilver mixed with The Dead, still gives me goosebumps. And yet, at that time, it was completely normal.

It is from this humus that this book was born. The idea, that is, that rock and politics are in any case linked, and from this point of view the music of the Grateful Dead is an excellent exemplification.

This bond, as it happens, has often characterized the friendships and discussions with many friends and comrades with whom I have exchanged political opinions and actions. The list would be endless, but I would like to thank some of them. Giorgio Griziotti and Massimiliano Guareschi read a first draft and helped improve its form. Salvo Leonardi, among the Dead's most knowledgeable music connoisseurs. Riccardo Bellofiore, with whom even on the musical side of psychedelic rock (he is more a Jefferson Airplane lover) I was able to express differences, and not only on economic theory. Alex Foti, who gave me an invaluable book as a gift: *The Deadheads Taping Compendium*. Giorgio Bonazzi, aka 'Mingus', and Carlo Cuccomarino (recently passed away), with whom I had the opportunity to exchange good music, good food and good vibes, and many others, including Matteo Tassinari, an expert music connoisseur.

I would also like to thank Piero Scaruffi, who has written exemplary pages on the music of the Grateful Dead.

Last but not least, I have to mention the Milano X publishing house, which published a first version in Italian, entitled *Grateful Dead Economy*, from which this English version is taken. In particular, I would like to thank Marco Philopat and Paoletta 'Nevrosi' Mezza.

A special thanks to Massimo De Angelis and to the Bloomsbury Academic team (in particular Atifa Jiwa), without whose help and support this book in English would not exist.

On the other hand, I cannot fail to thank Cristina, if only for the enormous patience and love she showed me in spending hours listening to the Grateful Dead's music without complaining too much.

This book is dedicated to our daughter Sole, so that she too may one day be spoilt for choice when faced with musical contributions of high innovative and social value. If that happens, it will mean that 'the times are a-changin'' (Bob Dylan).

P.S.: One final note. Every time I listen to Russian composer Pyotr Ilyich Tchaikovsky's Violin Concerto in D major op. 35 for pleasure, I cannot help but think how this extraordinary concerto anticipates the quintessence of psychedelic music. Listening to it, I can feel the same emotional vibrations as some live versions of the Grateful Dead's 'Dark Star', demonstrating, if proof were needed, that a certain kind of music, the kind that moves from subjectivities in conflict with themselves and the world around them, in a perpetual yearning for subversion and change, free of any commodification but an expression of the autonomy of thought and being, regardless of the modes and forms of execution, is united in the expression of the psyche and the human community in excess. I would like to remind you that the premiere of Tchaikovsky's concert in Vienna on 4 December 1881 was crushed in the *Neue Freie Presse* by the famous German critic Eduard Hanslick, whose view of the music was far removed from that of the Russian composer. Hanslick writes: 'Listening to the Tchaikovsky concerto, it occurred to me that there is such a thing as stinky music (stinkende Musik)'.

Here, this book is also dedicated to all 'stinky music', our music.

PREFACE TO THE ENGLISH EDITION

Introduction

Human history is made up of historical phases that follow one another in a way that is linear, by 'cycles and counter cycles of growth and decay',[1] and also emerges, always different, because each epoch is traversed by its own social and economic dialectics, that is, its own political culture. The phase we are currently experiencing is the one that marks the transition from the third technological revolution to the fourth. Very briefly, according to studies of the evolution of technical progress, which refer to Kondratief's long-wave theory,[2] the first technological (so-called 'industrial') revolution took place at the end of the eighteenth century in England and marked the start of the capitalist system with the French Revolution of 1789. This system is still the one we live in today, although it has undergone profound and structural changes from its origins in the early nineteenth century. The second technological leap is the one that marks the transition from craft capitalism to the Taylorist capitalism of the large factory at the beginning of the twentieth century. It is the birth of the figure of the mass worker[3] who replaces the craft worker, thanks to the exploitation of static economies of scale, able to foster high growth in industrial-manufacturing productivity (tangible production) and thus a higher rate of economic growth. The Taylorist and Fordist paradigm entered a crisis at the turn of the 1960s and 1970s due to

1. Cf. G. B. Vico, *Principj di una Scienza Nuova Intorno alla Natura delle Nazioni* ... (Naples: Felice Mosca) (in Italian). English version: *The New Science of Giambattista Vico*, translated by T. G. Bergin and M. H. Fisch (London: Cornell University Press, 1984).

2. N. Kondratiev, *The Long Wave Cycle*, translated by G. Daniels. Introduction by J. Snyder (New York: Richardson & Snyder, 1984).

3. The mass worker is the unskilled assembly line worker. Cf. S. Bologna, 'The Theory and History of the Mass Worker in Italy', *Common Sense* 11/12 (1987). Available online: https://libcom.org/article/theory-and-history-mass-worker-italy-sergio-bologna.

the excessive rigidity of production and technological organization and the saturation of demand for durable goods in the dominant sectors. This was the beginning of the third technological revolution (Information Communication Technology), partially the subject of this book, which for the first time in the history of capitalism saw the accumulation process increasingly focus on intangible production at the expense of industrial-material production. The new paradigm not only disrupts economic organization but also introduces new factors of valorization, such as the virtual space created by the internet, learning and social relations. Work itself changes structurally, requiring new skills both in terms of training and human social cooperation. The relationship between human being and machines begins to change. It still remains a relationship between different and separate inputs, but work performance is no longer a mere appendage of the machine, it increasingly requires the utilization of the workers' vital skills and faculties. The machine tends to become cognitive and talking, albeit with very crude alphabets, and requires interlocution with the human brain, senses and memory.

The ICT paradigm fosters the process of internationalization of production and sets in motion new techniques for financing accumulation activity (financialization) in a context in which the global financial order is disrupted by the collapse of the Bretton Woods system and money becomes pure digital money, losing all connection with physical matter (gold). Its value is increasingly determined by the speculative conventions acted out from time to time by international financial companies that increasingly centralize the management and control (but not the ownership) of huge virtual liquid sums in a few hands.

Currently, technological evolution seems to be moving towards the definition of a new technological paradigm, which some call the fourth industrial revolution.[4] There are several signs that things are moving in this direction. Without wishing to be exhaustive, we can note that in the last decade we have witnessed an increase in moments of economic and social crisis, especially in the aftermath of the severe global financial crisis of 2007–8. Moreover, on the technological front, we are witnessing an acceleration of innovative capacity, now increasingly directed and

4. Cf. K. Schwab, *The Fourth Industrial Revolution* (London: Penguin Books, 2017).

commanded by large international corporations, both in the West and East of the world.

This innovative capacity moves mainly in three directions.

The first has to do with the technologies of life, bio-technologies. Since the discovery at the beginning of the new millennium that there is an alphabet of life (the decryption of the human genome) and then in 2012 the discovery of how to decipher and alter it (the discovery of the molecular scissors CRISPR/Cas9), we are faced with a swarm of innovations that ultimately open the field to the possibility of creating artificial living material in the laboratory. These are revolutionary discoveries on a par with Russian chemist Mendeleev's periodic tables of the natural elements, which gave impetus to the development of inorganic chemistry and the possibility of creating artificial materials, without which the Taylorist technological wave would never have taken off.

At the same time, thanks to algorithmic technology and nanotechnology, the last few years have seen an exponential increase in the capacity to calculate, manage, manipulate and organize an increasing amount of data and information in ever smaller spaces, leading to the creation of cloud and big data technologies, thanks to which platform capitalism can flourish. This dynamic has also significantly affected the organization of work and productive and financial governance. In this regard, we can now say that the 'platform' model has penetrated as an organizational mode in all strategic sectors of contemporary accumulation. By platform model, we mean the existence of a digital infrastructure that plays an intermediary role in economic and social exchange relations. This technological infrastructure is made possible by new communication tools (e.g. smartphone and iPhone) and algorithms. This model makes it possible to value the everyday acts of life, without necessarily going through the intermediation of a certified work performance.[5]

The third trend, on the other hand, concerns the development of hybrid human-machine technologies, today increasingly present in the semi-automated learning processes of machine learning and deep-learning technologies, capable of creating the conditions for 'intelligent' automation, the short-term perspective of which is mainly represented by artificial intelligence (Internet of Thing, Industry 4.0, etc.).

5. On this point, we will elaborate further.

These three trends are mutually synergetic and feed off each other, thus fostering the development of an innovative cluster, typical of the emergence of a new technological paradigm.

On the other hand, it is entirely premature to discuss the technological trajectory(s) that may emerge from the new technological paradigm. On the one hand, the whole environmental question arises, on the other hand, the management of life. Zoe (biological life) and Bios (human life) are increasingly closely linked.

The emergence of the commonwealth

The spread of the ICT paradigm has profoundly changed the organization of work. It was after the first Gulf War that innovations in the field of transport and in the field of language and communication (ICTs) began to coalesce around a single new paradigm of accumulation and valorization. The new capitalist configuration tends to identify the commodity 'knowledge' and 'space' (geographical and virtual) as the new cornerstones on which to base an accumulation capacity. Thus, two new dynamic economies of scale are being determined that underpin productivity growth (and thus a source of valorization): learning economies and network economies. The former is linked to the process of generation and creation of new knowledge (on the basis of new communication and information technologies), the latter is derived from district organizational modes (territorial networks or system-areas), no longer used only for the production and distribution of goods, but increasingly as a vehicle for the dissemination (and control) of knowledge and technological progress.

The centrality of learning and network economies, typical of cognitive capitalism, was called into question with the beginning of the new millennium following the bursting of the 'Net-Economy' speculative bubble in March 2000. The new cognitive paradigm alone cannot guarantee the socio-economic system from its structural instability. New liquidity must be injected into the financial markets. In fact, the ability of financial markets to generate 'value' is linked to the development of 'conventions' (speculative bubbles) capable of creating homogeneous expectations that drive the main financial operators to bet on certain types of financial assets.[6] In the 1990s it was the Net Economy, in the 2000s the attraction came from the development of

6. Cf. A. Orléan, *De l'euphorie à la panique: penser la crise financière* (Paris: Cepremap, Editions Rue d'Ulm, 2009).

Asian markets (with China joining the WTO in December 2001) and real estate. In the recent period, it has focused on the dismantling of European welfare following the imposition of draconian austerity policies. Regardless of the type of dominant convention, contemporary capitalism is perpetually in search of new social and vital spheres to engulf and commodify, to the point of increasingly affecting the vital faculties of human beings. This is why, in recent years, we have begun to speak of bio-economy and bio-cognitive capitalism.[7]

With the advent of platforms, the commodification and direct valorization of life find their organizational model.

Network economies increasingly address the sphere of social reproduction, not just the development of learning faculties. Network economies presuppose the existence of social cooperation capable of expressing a general intellect.[8] While this social cooperation was

7. Cf. A. Fumagalli and C. Morini, 'Life Put to Work: Towards a Theory of Life-Value', *Ephemera* 10, no. 3/4 (2011): 234–52; C. Morini, *Per amore o per forza. Femminilizzazione del lavoro e biopolitiche del corpo* (Verona: Ombre Corte, 2010); A. Fumagalli and C. Morini, 'Cognitive Bio-capitalism, Social Reproduction and the Precarity Trap: Why Not Basic Income?', *Knowledge Cultures* 1, no. 4 (2013): 106–26; A. Fumagalli, S. Lucarelli, E. Musolino and G. Rocchi, 'Digital Labour in the Platform Economy', *Sustainability* 10 (2018): article 1757; A. Fumagalli, 'Bio-Cognitive Capitalism', in B. Skeggs, S. R. Farris, A. Toscano and S. Bromberg (eds), *The SAGE Handbook of Marxism*, vol. 3 (2022), Chapter 84, 1537–55.

8. The concept of general intellect is derived from a famous quotation in the 'Fragment on Machines' within Marx's *Grundrisse*. The general intellect represents the capacity of the human being and the cognitive machine to be a primary productive factor, the outcome of the social individual's cooperation processes. This definition, as Virno notes, differs from the Marx's definition. For Marx, general intellect 'is the knowledge objectified in fixed capital and embedded in the automated system of machinery'. Today the machinery is represented by the 'algorithm', a 'machine' that is born of workers' cooperation, of logistical intellectuality that the capital imposes over this cooperation, over precisely this massified intellectuality. With reference to the general intellect, it is possible to hypothesize a third form of subsumption. A. Negri writes: 'We can in fact state here, starting from the continuity of the subsumption process, from "formal" to "real", a third form of subsumption of society into capital, the "subsumption into the General Intellect"'. While formal subsumption refers to capitalist command of labour processes that originate outside of or prior to the capital relation, and real subsumption refers to the labour process internally

initially able to organize itself autonomously and thus could potentially be pitted against capital, the spread of platforms and the strict rules of access and processing of data (also in the name of privacy) have greatly reduced this autonomous capacity for self-determination of life.

Today, platform capitalism, thanks to the new technological paradigm based on cloud computing, nano-technologies, artificial intelligence and living bio-technologies, captures, selects, integrates, analyses and extracts a value from human relationships, thanks to *business intelligence*[9] functions. What is relevant is that this value, in relation to other values, presents itself as *exchange value*.

Unconsciously, human cooperation becomes an essential productive factor for the current accumulation process. We call this wealth of vital activity the 'commonwealth'. Today, the 'commonwealth' is the transposition of the general intellect on an enlarged scale, it represents the main factor of wealth generation, the expropriation of which by private corporations becomes the most important source of valorization and profit.

We can say, quoting Carlo Vercellone, that the commonwealth becomes a mode of production. It is in this definition that the difference between the commonwealth and the commons is defined and the major difference between the Italian Theory approach and the Anglo-Saxon approach is created.

Carlo Vercellone writes about the commonwealth as a mode of production:

reorganized to meet the dictates of capital, the subsumption into the general intellect refers to the capacity of capital to exploit the social cooperation. Negri adds: 'The formation of the General Intellect – as we know – corresponds to the structural crisis of industrial capitalism, brought about by workers' struggles (without underestimating the already important qualitative preponderance of knowledge in the living labour embedded in fixed capital)' (A. Negri, 'General Intellect and Social Individual in the Marxian Grundrisse', 2019. Available online: http://www.euronomade.info/?p=12059). It is the social individual, i.e. life itself, that becomes the object of this new type of subsumption, which is added, in a hybrid way, to the real and formal subsumption, already excised by Marx in *Capital*. Hence, it is possible to speak of 'life subsumption'. Cf. A. Fumagalli, *Economia Politica del Comune, Sfruttamento e sussunzione vitale nel capitalismo biocognitivo* (Rome: DeriveApprodi, 2019).

9. Cf. T. Davenport, *Big Data at Work: Dispelling the Myths, Uncovering the Opportunities* (Boston: Harvard Business Review Press, 2013).

The common [commonwealth[10]] is thus a product of a social and institutional construction that elects it to this status. It refers not to an essence that precedes it, but to the forms of governance and labour cooperation that insures its production, reproduction and distribution. Since it is so, the common potentially concerns every type of resource, good and service, even if this does not mean overlooking the specific management problems that each of them may present.[11]

And more:

From this point of view, common thus appears above all to be a social construction founded on the spread of knowledge and self-governance of production and not an intrinsic feature of the nature of particular categories of good.[12]

The commonwealth is thus understood as the basis of contemporary accumulation and the platform is the instrument of its governance.

In the book before you, the story is told of an experience of self-production and experimentation in the field of music represented by the Grateful Dead community. Its parable (and its defeat) is emblematic of the process of dispossession that the commonwealth, the outcome of the conflicts of the 1960s and 1970s, has undergone from the liberalist involution of the late 1980s to the new hierarchical order imposed by platform capitalism, an organized form of bio-cognitive capitalism, which governs and subsumes our lives.

The concept of the commonwealth is thus distinct from the concept of the commons. The latter requires governance or the establishment of governance practices through the empowerment of local communities. Such practices are motivated by the presence of a common good that needs collective action to be managed. And this resource is presented as non-excludable and rival. The imposition of private property is thus

10. Vercellone calls 'common' (singular) what we call 'commonwealth'. In other words, 'common' and 'commonwealth' are synonymous.

11. C. Vercellone et al., 'Managing the Commons in the Knowledge Economy', Report D3.2, D-CENT (Decentralized Citizens ENgagement Technologies), European Project 2015 (2015), 24. Available online: http://dcent project.eu/wp-content/uploads/2015/07/D3.2-complete-ENG-v2.pdf.)

12. Vercellone et al., 'Managing the Commons in the Knowledge Economy'.

the outcome of a deliberate act to make rival what does not present itself as such. An example of this is the commodity of knowledge and that of virtual space, not by chance the two 'commodities' at the heart of the capitalist accumulation process today. Such commodities present themselves as abundant and are not subject to scarcity: knowledge the more it is exchanged, the more it spreads, and virtual space (that of the internet) is by definition borderless. To make such goods privately appropriable, it becomes necessary to introduce 'enclosures', limitations of use. This, not by chance, is precisely the role played by intellectual property rights.

The governance of the commons intersects with the change in the cultural paradigm with which public policies are constructed, which become increasingly 'contractualized' (where there is a transition from authority to agreement) and oriented towards a governance approach, increasingly characterized by an inclusive approach. This change is also the outcome of the counter-cultural movements that have animated the Western world since the mid-1960s. In some cases, this approach is institutionalized, as in the case of water, for example, which goes from being an unlimited resource (a public good, not excludable and not subtractable) to being considered as a common (a common good, with high exclusion difficulty and high subtractability) whose use is to be managed and regulated in a different way from what has been done so far.

In this context, the cultural change underway with regard to the management of the commons is intended to rethink the relationship between citizens and public administrations and the conditions for self-government. The underlying question is: how, in contemporary society, can citizens govern their common resources from below in a cooperative manner? Put another way, how can commoning[13] practices be developed?

However, the experience of recent years tells us that commoning is operating and diffusing in different fields, as in precariat struggle, climate activism, struggles for Unconditional Basic Income. But the power of co-optation of capital is still very strong. Even when a referendum is won to take the water resource away from private management (as happened in Italy in 2011, after the liberalization of water services in

---

13. Cf. M. De Angelis, *Omnia Sunt Communia. On the Commons and the Transformation to Postcapitalism* (London: Bloomsbury, 2017).

2008) and keep it public, this outcome is then not respected and we continue as if nothing had happened.

We live in difficult times. But also in times when the human capacity for self-determination is, paradoxically, very high. Precisely because of this, direct (precariousness and debt) and indirect (imaginary, promise, personal empowerment …) devices are more pervasive and subsuming. But we must always remember that human beings can live without capital while capital cannot exist without human labour power. The environmental crisis is there to prove it. It is up to us to create instances of 'commonism'.

Happy reading!

Chapter 1

COUNTERCULTURE AND CYBERCULTURE: THE 1960S VS 1990S

It is well known that the period of the 1960s in the United States represented a cultural and political turning point of considerable importance, a sign of a paradigm shift that has indelibly innervated the following decades to the present day.

The second half of the 1960s brought to maturity what literary and musical avant-gardes had begun to experiment with in the previous decade. The Beat movement, bebop first and then free jazz, played the role of incubator of the social conquests of the years to come and of that mighty movement of liberation of bodies and brains that swept across the US from East to West.

We were told the following: If President Kerr tried to get something more liberal out of the regents in his telephone conversation, why didn't he make some public statement to that effect? And the answer we received, from a well-meaning liberal, was the following: He said, 'Would you ever imagine the manager of a firm making a statement publicly in opposition to his board of directors?' That's the answer! Well, I ask you to consider: If this is a firm, and if the board of regents is the board of directors; and if President Kerr is the manager; then I'll tell you something. The faculty are a bunch of employees, and we're the raw material! But we're a bunch of raw materials that don't mean to behave any process upon us. Don't mean to be made into any product. Don't mean … Don't mean to end up being bought by some clients of the University, be they the government, be they industry, be they organized labor, be they anyone! We're human beings![1]

1. For further information, see H. Draper, *Berkeley: The New Student Revolt* (Chicago: Haymarket Books, 2020). The video of Savio's speech is available

It was 2 December 1964, around noon, sixty-one years ago. So spoke Mario Savio,[2] one of the student leaders of the Free Speech Movement (FSM)[3] at the University of Berkeley, California, across the bay from Oakland, the place that would see the birth of the Black Panther Party a few years later.

Mario Savio continued:

> There's a time when the operation of the machine becomes so odious, makes you so sick at heart, that you can't take part! You can't even passively take part! And you've got to put your bodies upon the gears and the wheels … upon the levers, upon all the apparatus, and you've got to make it stop! And you've got to indicate to the people who run it, to the people who own it, that unless you're free, the machine will be prevented from working at all![4]

online: https://www.americanrhetoric.com/speeches/mariosaviosproulhallsitin. htm.

2. Son of an emigrant from Santa Caterina Villarmosa (province of Catania, Sicily, Italy), Mario Savio was one of the key figures in the Berkeley Free Speech Movement. Savio became a leading figure in the protest on the Berkeley campus on 1 October 1964: the university police officers had just put him in their car when he managed to climb onto the roof of the police car and give a speech that delighted the crowd. He died in Californian Sebastopol on 6 November 1996 at the age of fifty-four. See W. J. Rorabaugh, *Berkeley at War: The 1960s* (Oxford: Oxford University Press, 1989).

3. The Free Speech Movement (FSM) was a student protest movement that developed during the 1964–5 academic year on the campus of the University of California, Berkeley, under the informal leadership of students Mario Savio, Brian Turner, Bettina Aptheker, Steve Weissman, Art Goldberg, Jackie Goldberg and others. During the protests, unprecedented at the time, the students insisted that the university administration lift the campus ban on political activities and recognize the students' right to free speech and academic freedom. See R. Cohen and R. E. Zelnik, *The Free Speech Movement: Reflections on Berkeley in the 1960s* (University of California Press, 2002).

4. See Draper, *Berkeley: The New Student Revolt*, 165. Following this speech, Mario Savio came into the crosshairs of the FBI's 'charitable' care, at the instigation of the director himself, Edgar J. Hoover, creator of the COINTELPRO (an acronym for COunterINTELligencePROgram), which was aimed at annihilating, even physically, any opposition in the USA. On Savio, see http:// www.sfgate.com/bayarea/article/Thousands-of-runners-set-off-in-S-F-Marat hon-5649871.php. On COINTELPRO, responsible for some cold-blooded

After this speech, a thousand students poured into Sproul Hall, the building on the Berkeley campus where the administrative offices and the university president, Clark Kerr, were located, effectively occupying it with an unprecedented sit-in for the US university system. Inside, courses were immediately organized, giving rise to the 'Free University of California', a mode of action that became a leitmotif in following university occupations, including those in Europe in the following years. The occupation lasted until 3.30 a.m. the following day. At the request of the 'liberal' governor of California, Edmund G. Brown,[5] more than 500 policemen in riot gear burst onto the campus and arrested almost 800 students, who were passively resisting. The operation ends twelve hours later, leading to the largest mass arrest in American history.

After the Berkeley uprising, in the years that followed, the student movement became increasingly organized both theoretically and politically, starting with the birth of the SDS (Students for a Democratic Society), the Port Huron Declaration of 1965, the Columbia University uprising, the birth of the Weathermen and the large anti-war demonstrations in the spring of 1970, which had their tragic epilogue at Kent State University with the murder of four students by US military forces.

At the same time, the Afro-American and Indian movements also began to organize themselves and become the bearers of processes of liberation and social emancipation, starting with the Black Panther Party up to the Indian Liberation Movement.

* * * * *

The Berkeley uprising marks a watershed in the history of American social movements from the post-war period onwards. It was the mother of the counter-cultural movements of the 1960s that swept through not only the US but also Europe. And in Savio's discourse, there are already present the germs that would grow and be cultivated later: the denunciation against the disciplining of the university as a military-industrial complex (moreover involved, at that time, in the Cold

murders, such as that of Black Panther leader Fred Hampton in Chicago on 4 December 1969, see W. Churchill and J. V. Watt (eds), *Agents of Repression. The FBI's Secret War Against the Black Panther Party and the American Indian Movement* (Boston: South End Press, 1988).

5. To the press, Brown declares: 'We cannot come to terms with revolution, be it at the university or anywhere else'. Quoted in Draper, *Berkeley: The New Student Revolt*, 35.

War and only a little later in the American involvement in Vietnam); the denunciation against the rigid organization of studies that made students become a mere cog in an assembly line of knowledge.[6] In other words, the denunciation against the biopower (to quote Foucault) of a disciplinary nature (to quote Deleuze) of the Fordist-Taylorist paradigm.

But Savio's and the Berkeley FSM's discourse goes further: in a still confusing way (they were then referring to a pre-digital, highly material production within factories made up of the gears, machinery and bodies of the mass worker), they allude to the term 'machine' concerning a context where information and information technology are beginning to play an increasingly important role. The 'machine' to which Savio alludes is not yet the computer but prefigures it.[7]

The struggle against the despotic rationalization of the 'machine' in favour of the recognition of the humanity of the individual thus represents the first step towards liberation from the technocracy imposed by Fordist industrial capital. This will be a theme that will be at the core of all subsequent movements and will also underpin the transition from Fordist capitalism to cognitive and bio-cognitive capitalism (platform capitalism).

* * * * *

Thirty-two years later, on 8 February 1996, John Perry Barlow, a computer journalist and digital technology expert, was in Davos to attend the meetings of the World Economic Forum, a summit that brings together the political-industrial establishment of the global oligarchy, from the president of the major capitalist nations to the CEOs of the globe's most important multinationals and leading financial experts and speculators; it will also be protested against by the post-Seattle no-global movement. Barlow was also known for being one of the main songwriters of the lyrics of the Grateful Dead, the Californian rock band that was the queen of psychedelic music in the San Francisco Sound in the 1960s and 1970s. Watching the CNN news, Barlow learned that the Telecommunication Act had been passed by Congress (with

6. Mario Savio himself stated in an interview that he and many other UC Berkeley students felt like 'little more than an IBM card'. See Draper, *Berkeley: The New Student Revolt*, 153. See M. Savio, 'California's Angriest Student', in *Life*, 26 February 1965, 100.

7. See F. Turner, *From Counterculture to Cyberculture* (Chicago: University of Chicago Press, 2006), 11ff.ff.

only five votes against), a law aimed at regulating communication on the internet and which contained the Communication Decency Act: under the pretext of restricting access to pornography on the internet, a series of constraints on language was introduced, with the risk of considerably limiting freedom of expression (free speech).

> Governments of the Industrial World, you weary giants of flesh and steel, I come from Cyberspace, the new home of Mind. On behalf of the future, I ask you of the past to leave us alone. You are not welcome among us. You have no sovereignty where we gather. We have no elected government, nor are we likely to have one, so I address you with no greater authority than that with which liberty itself always speaks. I declare the global social space we are building to be naturally independent of the tyrannies you seek to impose on us. You have no moral right to rule us nor do you possess any methods of enforcement we have true reason to fear.[8]

In this statement, the themes of freedom of expression already claimed by the Free Speech Movement in the 1960s are echoed. There is therefore a common thread linking these two moments thirty years apart. On the other hand, it cannot be otherwise, since in these thirty years the United States (and not only the United States) has gone through a period of strong social and economic transformations, characterized by two phases of strong social and cultural revolutions.

The first is the development of the counterculture of the late 1960s, which accelerated the crisis of the techno-military establishment that had characterized the growth and apogee of the Taylorist disciplinary paradigm and Fordist capitalism.

The second is the development of cyberculture in the 1990s, which accompanied the birth and spread – with all its contradictions – of the new paradigm of cognitive capitalism, based on the use of digital technologies, knowledge, the free circulation of knowledge, social cooperation, the general intellect, learning and network economies.

Two social and, above all, cultural movements that nevertheless present very different motivations, contents and historical contingencies (a technological revolution took place in the middle!), even though they are linked, however, by that yearning for individual (rather than

---

8. J. P. Barlow, 'Declaration of Independency of Cyberspace', Davos, Switzerland, 8 February 1996. Available online: http://www.eff.org/~barlow.

collective, unlike in Europe) freedom that is typical of the mentality and history of the United States, unified by the myth of the frontier.

As Fred Turner writes:

> For Barlow, digital technologies have ceased to represent the emblem of bureaucratic alienation and have instead become the tool with which bureaucracy and alienation can be overcome. Echoing the rhetoric of the WSF, Barlow argued that Americans are once again in the midst of a social revolution. But this time, the forces of information were on the side of the people.[9]

For Mario Savio, computers had the power to transform students' and people's bodies into inanimate processors (into 'drones') within factories subordinated to the unilateral power of a highly disciplined and militarized society. For Barlow, on the other hand, that same power empowered women and men to be part of a world that could enhance their identity and foster social cooperation. Once freed from the hierarchies imposed by the material world, the individuals of Barlow's cybernetic space will be able to imagine a society not too dissimilar from the one advocated by the Free Speech Movement, a society free of bureaucracy and hierarchies.

The information technology revolution and the development of the ICT paradigm completely changed the perception of technology, just as the Lysergic revolution of the late 1960s had completely changed the perception of individual freedom, which until then had been enclosed within the cages of the Fordist discipline. If human beings and machines were then antagonists, they now become allies, and the machine, a machine no longer made of levers, wheels, bolts, belts, noise and sweat, but a machine made of languages, relationships, processors, coding, calculation, standardization, memory and cooperation, is seen as a means, indeed as a 'medium', for the liberation of man.

For example, Esther Dyson, Silicon Valley journalist and entrepreneur, in her 1997 best-seller *Release 2.0: A Design for Living in the Digital Age*,[10] argued that the internet would soon dissolve the bureaucracy of markets, stripping individuals and businesses of material elements. In a virtual world, where borders are not drawn, both humans and

---

9. Turner, *From Counterculture to Cyberculture*, 13–14.

10. E. Dyson, *Release 2.0: A Design for Living in the Digital Age* (New York: Broadway Books, 1977).

businesses would become merely nodes of information, able to circulate freely and, given their quantity, difficult to control in bureaucratic and hierarchical structures.[11]

* * * * *

In the intervening thirty years, a Copernican revolution has, therefore, taken place. The paradigm of accumulation and organization of labour and society has structurally changed. Material production, based on the 'man-machine relationship', leaves more and more room for immaterial production, based on the 'man-knowledge' relationship. Physical capital – the machine – is transformed into human and intangible capital. Hybrids are created between materiality and immateriality, between physical body and intellect, which science fiction literature has already anticipated with the concept of 'cyborg' and 'replicant'.[12] The economic and social hierarchy based on ownership of the means of production (hence of the machine) of the post-war years tends to mutate into intellectual property. Money itself changes shape and the modalities of its circulation and issuance are modified. Money dematerializes completely and loses any link with the commodity, albeit a symbolic commodity such as gold might have been, turning into pure 'sign money' in the aftermath of the collapse of Bretton Woods agreements (15 August 1971). This is the beginning of the process of financialization that will develop fully in the 1990s, at the height of the digital revolution, which will lead financial markets and their oligarchies to become the heart of the accumulation and valorization of capitalism in the new millennium. Today we can say, even in the light of the economic and financial crisis that has swept the world since 2008, that new forms of hierarchies and despotism have been realized and have grown.

But in the mid-1990s (for the digital revolution), as well as in the mid-1960s (for the libertarian and pacifist movements), hopes and confidence were high with the possibility that a new humanity and a new sociality (could we say, a new ethics?) could become hegemonic and improve the living conditions of humanity.

Despite the stellar distance between these two eras, there is a trait union, a symbolic bridge, that unites them, in addition to the everlasting and immortal tension for freedom and human emancipation: this bridge is the music and community spirit of the Grateful Dead.

11. Turner, *From Counterculture to Cyberculture*, 14.
12. The film *BladeRunner* was released in 1982.

We refer not only to one of the best-known American rock groups, considered by many to be the greatest rock band of all time, a monument to San Francisco hippy civilization and, in general, a monument to the psychedelic civilization of the 1960s, but to that community spirit and philosophy of life that always accompanied them until the 1990s and the untimely death (in 1995) of their guru: Jerry Garcia.

And it is this philosophy of life based on a communicative spirit and libertarian social cooperation in a total break with the disciplinary devices of the time that made the Grateful Dead witness, participate and be involved in the main episodes that punctuated the transition from the counterculture of the 1960s to the cyberculture of the 1990s more than any other US group: we do not know how aware and fully conscious they were since they always claimed at the time (unlike other rock and soul groups, such as Jefferson Airplane, the MC5 or Sly and Family Stone, among others) the apolitical nature of their music and their social commitment.

In their early days, the Grateful Dead was the soundtrack in 1965–7 of Acid Tests, organized by Ken Kesey, the author of *Someone Flew Over the Cuckoo's Nest*, and the Merry Pranksters.

The Merry Pranksters were a movement born in 1962, in California, based on the hippy philosophy. They marked the transitional period between the Beat Generation and the birth of the hippy movement itself and were among the main proponents of the use of psychedelic substances, a practice that became widespread from the Summer of Love in 1967.[13] In the summer of 1964, they travelled across the United States on a school bus decorated with psychedelic designs (which became famous as the Magic Bus). Neal Cassidy, an emblematic figure of the Beat Generation and alter-ego of Dean Moriarty (the main character of Jack Kerouac's *On the Road*) was also part of it.[14] The Grateful Dead, from January 1966 onwards,[15] formed the soundtrack, and it was during these happenings that some of their most lysergic

---

13. D. Taylor, *It Was Twenty Years Ago Today* (New York: Random House, 1987).

14. T. Wolfe, *The Electric Kool-Aid Acid Test* (New York: Farrar Straus Giroux, 1968); D. Malvinni, *Grateful Dead and the Art of Rock Improvisation* (Plymouth: Scarecrow Press, 2013).

15. The first Acid Test featuring the Grateful Dead as backing band and musical basis took place on 8 January 1966 at the Fillmore Auditorium in San Francisco.

pieces came to life, such as 'Caution (Do Not Stop on Tracks)', which would become part of their second record, *Anthem of the Sun*. In one of the band's historic pieces, the long suite 'That's It for the Other One' (also released on *Anthem of the Sun*, music and lyrics by Jerry Garcia, Bob Weir and Bill Kreutzmann), the Acid Test period is recalled, making explicit reference to the 'Magic Bus' and Neal Cassidy, on a journey 'to never-ever land'.

References to the Merry Pranksters' 'Magic Bus' and Neal Cassidy are quite evident when it is acknowledged that it was there 'that it all began'. There is also another song from the 1970s (1972) in which there is an indirect reference to the Beat Generation and Neal Cassidy. The title is 'Cassidy', written by J. P. Barlow and set to music by Bob Weir, Grateful Dead guitarist, together with Jerry Garcia. The song is dedicated to Cassidy Law, the newborn daughter of Eileen Law, one of the group's first public relations women. In the lyrics, references to the two Cassidys overlap, even contrasting, almost as if to indicate a sort of intergenerational transition between the decade of the 1960s and the next. In this way, the Grateful Dead became the bridge from the Beat Generation to the Hippy Generation.[16]

During the student protests, while still declaring themselves apolitical, the Grateful Dead took part in the most significant events. On 23 April 1968, the students of Columbia University in New York, organized by the SDS (Students for a Democratic Society), began a non-violent occupation of the campus that lasted about a week to protest against the close ties between the administration and the university management with the industrial-military apparatus engaged in the war of aggression against Vietnam and against the expropriation of some land from the African-American community for the construction of a private university gymnasium in Morningside Park. The administration, as in Berkeley four years earlier, called in the police who intervened with much greater brutality, injuring many of the occupiers and arresting more than 700 students. During the strike that followed, which stopped

16. Several times Neal Cassidy and Allan Ginsberg themselves participated in live performances. Listen to the Grateful Dead's live performance at the Straight Theater, Haight Street, on 23 July 1967, where Cassidy raps (https:// archive.org/details/gd1967-07-23.sbd.bershaw-wulf.5418.shnf) or the live performance at Polo Field in San Francisco's Golden Gate Park during the Human-be-in on 14 January 1967 (https://archive.org/details/gd67-01-14.sbd. vernon.9108.sbeok.shnf).

all activity at the university, a free concert by the Grateful Dead[17] was also held in support of the students' struggle against the war in Vietnam and racial discrimination. Mark Rudd, one of the leaders of the protest and one of the founding members of the future Weathermen Underground, remembers the event as follows:

> Walking across campus in those weeks was like navigating through a revolutionary jamboree, with classes meeting under trees, guerrilla-theatre groups performing, music constantly being made, including a free performance by a small young band out of Palo Alto, California, named Grateful Dead.[18]

The spring of 1970 is remembered as a season in which the war in Vietnam reached one of its climaxes with the American invasion of Cambodia at the beginning of the year and the resurgence of internal repression against the pacifist and libertarian movement. In particular, during the second half of April and the beginning of May, the anti-war movement reached perhaps its highest spread and consensus with massive demonstrations in the capital and numerous strikes on university campuses. On 4 May 1970, at Kent State University in Ohio, the Civil Guard shot at unarmed students who were in a rally, murdering four of them.[19]

The Grateful Dead, touring universities in the north-east, responded to the repression with a free concert at MIT (Massachusetts Institute of Technology) in Boston, during which one of the best versions of 'Morning Dew' was played.

Despite problems with amplification, due to the improvisation of the event and the fact that the stage was outdoors in rather harsh

---

17. Photos of the event can be found at http://www.dead.net/tags/colum bia-university. Unfortunately, there is no recording of the concert, not even in the almost complete collection of all Grateful Dead live performances available on archive.org (https://archive.org/details/GratefulDead). Only excerpts are available: see http://vimeo.com/68564387. The Grateful Dead were the only rock band to play on campus during the protest.

18. M. Rudd, *Underground. My Life with SDS and Weather Underground* (New York: Harper Collins, 2009), 94.

19. The Ohio Deads were to be the subject of numerous rock music lyrics, starting with perhaps the most famous: 'Ohio', by the supergroup Crosby, Still, Nash & Young: https://www.youtube.com/watch?v=EFwDtTeeg9M.

temperatures, testimonies from the time tell us that the emotional impact of the performance was very strong and tensions very high. At MIT, this concert has become legendary.[20]

Here is the testimony of a student present, in the discussion on archive.org, after the live performance was published:

> Previous reviewer hits on the Kent State massacre and this concert being donated free on the M.I.T student union steps in support of Students and in remembrance of '4 dead in Ohio'. The tension level had to be extremely high with what has just transpired at Kent State and to me it just feels like especially with the very hot 'Dancin in the Streets' that the Dead are able to channel that anger vibe into a musical release. When Bobby (Weir, Ed.) starts to scream out, 'Come on their Dancing' it is so strong it ends up being sobering. (Let cooler heads prevail). Everyone talks about all the great things that happened in the 60's well they were some very intense times as well.[21]

Two days earlier, the Grateful Dead played at Wesleyan University, a university college attached to Yale University in New Haven in Upstate New York, for a benefit in support of the release of eight members of the Black Panthers in Chicago, and Bobby Seale, one of the leaders of the Black Panther Party. Here is one spectator's witness:

> I was at the Wesleyan concert on May 3, 1970, which took place on a Sunday night (it was originally booked as a Sunday afternoon concert, but the Dead got that wrong) and on the next day, Monday May 4, four were dead in Ohio. Yale University was on strike to protest the expansion of the war in Cambodia, but Wesleyan was not on strike at that point … I …. recall that Weir and Garcia hit the stage and did some acoustic things while waiting for the rest of the band to show up … At Wesleyan University, we are talking about a small corner of the ball field/quads, a small stage that was not elevated, it was a very

20. The recording of the concert can be heard at https://archive.org/deta ils/gd1970-05-06.sbd.gans-hall.95.shnf (Cambridge, MA: Kresge Plaza, MIT). Here is the setlist of songs: 'Dancin' in The Streets', 'China Cat Sunflower – I Know You Rider', 'Next Time You See Me', 'Morning Dew', 'Good Lovin" – Drums, 'Good Lovin", 'Casey Jones', 'St. Stephen', 'Not Fade Away'.

21. See Deadlist forum: https://archive.org/details/gd1970-05-06.sbd. gans-hall.95.shnf.

intimate show that ended in the night, and as they finished, a man grabbed the microphone and told all in the audience not to forget about Bobby Seale, the Chicago Eight, the war … The following day, even Wesleyan was on strike.[22]

This testimony also allows us to analyse the relationship between the Grateful Dead and the African-American movements of the time, in particular the Black Panther Party. One of the leaders of the Black Panthers, Huey P. Newton, had the opportunity to meet Jerry Garcia, Grateful Dead guitarist, on a flight from San Francisco to New York in September 1970. Garcia recalled that meeting as follows:

We had a long and pleasant conversation. We liked each other and I was favorably impressed by him. We thought that if there was something to be done, we could do it for him, or, at least, try to do it.

The Black Panthers had long had contacts with San Francisco Bay Area musicians. Jefferson Airplane attended several benefits organized in support of the Black Panthers (before the band became Jefferson Starship). Among the most frequent were also the Grateful Dead, who on a couple of occasions opened for the Panthers' band, The Lumpen. Particularly significant was the concert on 5 March 1971 in Oakland, near San Francisco, headquarters of the Black Panther Party as well as their hometown, on the occasion of leader H. P. Newton's birthday. This was the official confirmation of the close link between the psychedelic group and the main African-American struggle organization. On this occasion, according to witnesses, the members of the Black Panthers left their weapons in the wardrobe and attended the concert unarmed, showing their respect for the band.

In an interview after the show, Garcia confirmed their desire to remain apolitical:

We have some loose semi-association with the Black Panthers because we met Huey and got along well with him. We don't deal with things based on content, the idea of a philosophy, or any of that **** – mostly it's personalities. The show did what it was supposed to do – it made them some bread. [He added that the Dead admired

22. See Deadlists forum: https://archive.org/details/gd70-05-03.aud.cots man.9378.sbeok.shnf.

some of the Panthers' programs, like the free breakfasts for children.]
But it's not our concern what they're doing or why they're doing it.[23]

Needless to say, after this meeting, the Grateful Dead came under the spotlight of Hoover's FBI and COINTELPRO,[24] who were already investigating the group for drug use (which is hardly surprising!), following the outlawing of LSD on 6 October 1966.

The apolitical nature of the Grateful Dead's music was confirmed in words, but not in deeds. Jerry Garcia's endorsement of social service activities (such as free breakfasts for black children) was nothing more than the legacy of the Haight-Ashbury hippy philosophy of post-1966 San Francisco, when the Diggers, the most politicized part of the hippy movement (in the person of Dr David E. Smith), founded the Haight Ashbury Free Clinic on 7 June 1967. In this clinic, everyone living in the neighbourhood (and beyond) could receive free treatment, and it was so successful that it became a model for other similar experiences. Numerous benefit concerts were organized by the Grateful Dead (and other groups from the Bay Area, such as Jefferson Airplane and the Quicksilver Messenger Service) to support the clinic's care activities, in a community spirit of solidarity that has always characterized the hippy philosophy and the Grateful Dead themselves.[25] Today, truly one of a kind, the Free Clinic in Haight-Ashbury is still in operation.

Once the counterculture period of the late 1960s was over and the ebb towards hedonism and yuppieism of the 1980s began, the Grateful Dead still maintained their community spirit. In the 1970s

23. P. Doggett, *There's A Riot Going On. Rock Stars, and the Rise and Fall of 60s Counter-Culture* (Edinburgh: Canongate Books, 2008), 411.

24. COINTELPRO was a series of covert and illegal projects actively conducted by the United States Federal Bureau of Investigation (FBI) aimed at surveilling, infiltrating, discrediting, and disrupting domestic American political organizations: https://en.wikipedia.org/wiki/COINTELPRO.

25. In the double live *Live Dead* of February 1969, which reproduces some evenings recorded at the Avalon Ballroom and the Fillmore West in San Francisco on 26 January and 27 February 1969 respectively, there are some photos of live performances by the Grateful Dead on Ashbury or Haight Street in support of the Free Clinic. The Grateful Dead had a small truck that served as a stage and on whose doors amplifiers were mounted so that they could play live on any street or square. For example, https://archive.org/details/gd1968-03-03. aud.finney.5809.sbeok.shnf.

and 1980s, the group played numerous live concerts at very low prices and where it was possible to record their performances for free. These were real happenings with long improvisation jams over four hours. The event was not only the concert and listening to the music but also everything around it. Each concert was followed by a throng of fans – the Deadheads – who attended every date of the tour, moving from city to city, stadium to stadium, to attend all the band's concerts. One of the characteristics of the Grateful Dead was that hardly any live show was the same as another. The component of musical improvisation was so high that the same pieces were played with different versions and varying lengths. Consequently, especially in the United States, the Grateful Dead were known for their live performances, the listening to which, constantly recorded and available on cassettes and tapes that passed from hand to hand, was the basis of a real veneration, a sort of almost religious cult that generated a real ethic of the common, of mutual solidarity and exchange often outside of a mercantile logic. The 1973 and 1974 tours, with concerts lasting on average over four hours (with versions of some pieces lasting over twenty-five minutes),[26] were recorded almost in their entirety, taking advantage of recordings made by both the group's sound engineers and the audience themselves. The recordings are usually of good quality, considering that at the time the development of digital and recording techniques were completely non-existent. The reason is simple: the Grateful Dead, who were always very concerned about the purity of sound, were great innovators in live amplification techniques. Since they were never satisfied with the

26. On the website https://archive.org/details/GratefulDead, all concerts from 1973 and 1974 can be downloaded for free and listened to. For 1973 only: live at Dane County Coliseum on 15 February 1973 (3 h 30 mins); live at William and Mary College Hall on 11 September 1973 (3 h 23 mins); live at Winterland Arena on 11 November 1973 (three consecutive evenings at Winterland in San Francisco), the recordings of which are now collected in a nine-CD booklet: *Winterland 1973: The Complete Recordings*; live at Pauley Pavilion – University of California on 17 November 1973 (with a medley of 'Playing in the Band', 'Uncle's John Band', 'Morning Dew' of almost fifty minutes); live at Denver Coliseum on 20 November 2013; live at Seattle Center Arena on 26 June 1973 (3 h 40 mins). All the concerts and various recordings are also commented and referenced in M. Getz and J. R. R. Dwork (eds), *The Deadheads Taping Compendium, vol. I, 1959–74* (New York: Owl Books, 1998). I thank Alex Foti for procuring me a copy of this valuable book.

systems they found on site at the venues where they played, they asked their sound engineer Owsley 'Bear' Stanley to design a special monitor system. The Dead used this system until the early 1970s when Stanley was jailed for manufacturing and selling LSD. The group then turned to Alembic Inc. studios to have an unprecedented amplification system built, known as the Wall of Sound. Dan Healy, Mark Raizene, Ron Wickersham, Rick Turner, John Curl of Alembic Inc. and, when he was released from prison in 1972, Stanley himself worked on the system.

The purpose of the Wall of Sound was to achieve undistorted amplification provided by a system that could also function as a monitor. It consisted of eleven independent amplification subsystems. Each instrument had its channel and its own set of separate amplification boxes. Phil Lesh's bass even had a channel for each string, and, similarly, there was a different channel for different elements of the drums. In this way, the sound of each instrument was extremely clean and there was no distortion due to intermodulation between instruments. The speaker system was positioned behind the instrumentalists, allowing them to hear exactly what the audience was hearing. To prevent this from generating feedback, a special microphone system was also designed. For each singer there was a pair of microphones at a distance of 60 mm and out of phase: the singer used the top microphone, and all signals in both microphones (i.e. the sound from the Wall of Sound that would produce the feedback) were automatically eliminated.

When the band took a break from live concerts in late 1974, the Wall of Sound was disassembled. In 1976, the Grateful Dead replaced it with a less expensive and complex amplification system.[27]

This amplification system also allowed some thirty microphones to be directly connected to the PA system so that live recordings could be made by members of the audience who had a tape recorder. These recordings gave rise to a very large number of bootlegs, which circulated freely with the consent of the band members themselves, who indeed, unlike other rock bands, bound by intellectual property rights clauses, encouraged their dissemination. In an *ante litteram* manner, the Grateful Dead were certainly the first rock group of international stature that, before the digital era and YouTube, promoted 'free music'. In this regard, this early form of the commons (music as a common good) never favoured the sale of studio records that never climbed to the top of the charts, but allowed each Grateful Dead concert to have

27. See http://en.wikipedia.org/wiki/Grateful_Dead.

an average audience of over 50,000, many of whom were non-paying or paying very little. It is therefore not surprising that at the end of the two-year period 1973–4 (when there were over 300 live performances), the economic result was not at all positive![28]

However, this attitude towards the free enjoyment of the group's live music did not spread without contradictions, clashes and disputes. It was only at the end of the 1960s and the beginning of the 1970s that some Deadheads started to secretly record some concerts. Despite the limited means at their disposal, the results turned out to be excellent. Thus began a black market in tapes: recordings which were obviously illegal under American law, especially since the Grateful Dead had a recording contract with Warner Bros.[29] It was especially during the two-year period of the big Wall of Sound concerts that this market began to flourish, creating problems for the Grateful Dead themselves, both from the point of view of legality but also from an economic point of view. Some members of the band's crew (as opposed to the band members)[30] began to check for 'pirate' recordings and to confiscate any recordings. But the results were disappointing, to the point that from the late 1970s onwards, the practice of pirate recordings became effectively unstoppable. The conclusion was – as always happens when a practice initially considered illegal becomes mainstream – that not only were recordings allowed but they were also assisted by technical support.

The writer has directly observed that 30–40 metres in front of the stage, a special area was set up with a certain number of microphones, directly connected to the mixer, available for those who wanted to record the concert with their equipment.[31] This practice has resulted

28. The Grateful Dead's financial situation at the end of 1974 was dire, not least because the Revd Lenny Hart, father of drummer Mickey Hart, escaped with the $300,000 cash box of concert income. The cost of maintaining and transporting the Wall of Sound and the low record sales could not be compensated for by the income from live concerts. It must also be taken into account that the Grateful Dead constituted a family/commune of many people, whose livelihood depended solely on the band.

29. The Grateful Dead were the last San Francisco Bay Area group to be put under contract.

30. D. G. McNally, *A Long Strange Trip. The inside history of The Grateful Dead* (New York: Three Rivers Press, 2003), 375.

31. Live concert 10 July 1989, Giants Stadium, New York: https://archive.org/details/gd89-07-10.sbd.16071.sbeok.shnf.

in the incredible spread of the Grateful Dead cult over the last thirty years and the possibility, as already mentioned, of having over 6,000 live concert recordings, a record that no rock band will ever be able to boast.

It was therefore during the 1980s that the Grateful Dead's music spread outside the more strictly commercial circuits. Can we talk about an experiment/institution of the commonwealth? It is difficult to answer, not least because in the meantime a parallel merchandising market developed that still represents an important source of income for the group's – capitalistic – economic activities.

However, the communitarian and libertarian spirit persists and so it is not surprising that, albeit indirectly, the Grateful Dead, or rather their ethos, is still present on 8 February 1996, the day of the Declaration of Independence of Cyberspace, drafted by J. P. Barlow, not coincidentally the author of lyrics to many Grateful Dead songs (including the aforementioned 'Cassidy') in common with guitarist Bob Weir, an old friend, whom they met in high school in the early 1960s. And it is not surprising that this statement is dedicated to the memory of Jerry Garcia, who died the previous year.

The spirit of music as a common is translated and revived in the concept of cyberspace as a common.

* * * * *

In this essay, we intend to use the metaphor of the Grateful Dead not only to pay tribute to one of the rock groups that has most affected alternative culture and it is very little known in Italy, but also to critically discuss the evolution of the libertarian spirit in the United States, born and developed in the 1960s and merged in the last two decades in the 'libertarian' ideology, based prominently on individual freedom, anti-statism and the primacy of the spirit of the self-made man. And how this transition has been very functional, on the one hand, as the driving force behind high-tech digital innovation and, on the other, the spirit of knowledge neo-capitalism.

In the second chapter, we will present a more detailed analysis of the music of the Grateful Dead, and then, in the following three chapters, we will analyse in greater depth some concepts that are today at the centre of the alternative political debate of the new millennium: the concept of the commune, the open-source spirit against intellectual property rights for the free use of knowledge, the role of money as a pure sign and its alternative implications, and the self-organization of living labour.

The key to the interpretation we want to offer is this: this process of capturing the libertarian spirit for capitalist purposes has been handed down from the 1960s to the present day, passing through the cognitive and digital revolutions of the 1990s. Today, this process represents one of the clearest examples of life subsumption, an inherently ambiguous concept that warrants future study. On the one hand, it recognizes that the life of individuals, at the very moment it triggers processes of social cooperation, can be a harbinger of subversive behaviour that is often legally disruptive. On the other hand, this potential subversion frequently becomes one of the most powerful levers of today's capitalist valorization.

Chapter 2

THE MUSIC OF THE GRATEFUL DEAD[1]

Grateful Dead are more well known within the USA than elsewhere. Yet they are considered by many to be the greatest rock band of all time,[2] a monument of San Francisco's hippy civilization and, in general, a monument of the psychedelic culture of the 1960s.

During those years, the Grateful Dead lived in a sort of commune, consisting of more than twenty people, in the centre of the Haight-Ashbury district, at 710 Ashbury Street, in a beautiful two-storey Victorian-style house with a classic staircase in the entrance hall and a garden in front, built mostly of wood. They always had an image as being unrepentant freaks, which they carried with them for many years. Even in the late 1980s, the Deadheads (as the band's fans were called) would pitch tents, sell chillum, eat macrobiotic food and walk naked around the concert grounds (when the weather and temperature permitted), recreating a Woodstock or Watkins Glen[3] atmosphere in the style of the hippy festivals of the 1960s and early 1970s. And yet, despite this

1. For these notes, I make full use of the writing on the Grateful Dead available on Piero Scaruffi's blog, 1990, who I cordially thank for his timely and convincing critical analysis: http://www.scaruffi.com/vol2/grateful.html.

2. Cf. http://www.scaruffi.com/vol2/grateful.html.

3. We are referring to the Summer Jam Festival in Watkins Glen on 28 July 1973, when the Grateful Dead played together with The Allman Brothers Band and The Band, in front of an estimated 600,000 people, the largest audience ever to attend a live concert. The day before at 10.15 a.m., during the rehearsal of the PA system, the Grateful Dead performed one of their most beautiful jams/improvisations of almost 20′, which became known as the *Soundcheck Jam*, today listenable in its entirety in the five-CD box: *So Many Roads*, Grateful Dead Records, November 1999 (which contains, among other things, other beautiful jams).

cliché that, especially in the 1960s, disturbed the quiet, bourgeois way of life, the Grateful Dead were one of the most erudite ensembles of their time, educated as much in the European and American atonal avant-garde as in the modal improvisations of free jazz, and in the rhythms of other cultures, capable of transforming feedback and unusual metres into the equivalent of chamber instruments. Few rock musicians have performed such a cultured operation in the jam form.[4]

Their greatest invention was, in fact, the long piece of group improvisation, the rock equivalent of the jazz jam. Unlike jazz, in which the jam sublimated the anguish of the Afro-American people, the Grateful Dead's jams were the expression of a libertarian culture, certainly lysergic, which expressed (or, rather, wanted to express) a sort of escape from the System, expressive freedom, an alternative life. The infinite ascending and descending scales of Jerry Garcia, the group's guru, are among the most titanic feats attempted by rock music.[5]

The Grateful Dead of those years sold only a few records. Their form of expression was the live show, not the record, which was too rigid a format to encapsulate their improvisations. Suffice it to mention their most famous live works (among the masterpieces of rock history): *Live Dead*, the group's first double album, released in November 1969, consists of three sides ([Side A: 'Dark Star', 23' 07"]; [Side B: 'St. Stephen', 6' 32"; 'The Eleven' 9' 19"]; [Side C: 'Turn on Your Love Light', 15' 08"]) that represent a 54' 06" continuum of music without interruption, which could only be heard on CD without having to interrupt the music to turn the vinyl over. In this sense, the Dead surpassed another commercial format: if the album was the format of choice for non-commercial musicians and represented a form of rebellion against the entire marketing apparatus of popular music (based on the fast enjoyment of the 45 rpm), the concert rejected the laws of advanced capitalism altogether, relegating the business plan to second place.

The Grateful Dead's early concerts were big free parties, where the entrance fee (when there was one) only paid for the venue's costs. Even afterwards, the Grateful Dead would always have preferred to perform live rather than encode their 'songs' on vinyl. In this sense there is no definitive version of their songs, there are only versions on disc and versions that did not end up on disc. In this sense, the Grateful Dead

4. Cf. http://gratefuldeadprojects.com/Jam_Segments.html.

5. Cf. D. Malvinni, *Grateful Dead and the Art of Rock Improvisation* (Plymouth: Scarecrow Press, 2013).

revolutionized the concept of rock music in the same way that jazz had revolutionized the European concept of music in general with the idea that music could be improvised. Many jams did not have a name but only a progressive number. Of these, the best known is *Eleven* (published in *LiveDead*), but there is also *Seven* (never published on record). Of these, some became known by the names that Deadheads themselves had coined in even imaginative ways, *Mountain Jam* (possibly named after a verse by Donovan: 'There Is a Mountain'), *Beautiful Jam*, *Clementine Jam* and the already mentioned *Soundcheck Jam*, or they referred back to already existing pieces such as *Spanish Jam* (from the reference to the song 'Solea' played by Miles Davis on the album *Sketches of Spain*), *Mind Left Body Jam* (referring to a piece by Paul Kantner of Jefferson Starship, entitled 'Your Mind Has Left Your Body' from the album *Baron von Tollbooth & the Chrome Nun*), *Feelin' Groovy Jam* (from the well-known Simon & Garfunkel song), The *Main Ten Jam* (which would turn into one of the Dead's hits, 'Playing in the Band'), *Darkness Jam* (from a Youngbloods song), 'Nobody's Fault but Mine' (from a well-known blues, often played by Blind Willie Johnson), to name but a few.[6]

Their free-themed jams actually arose from the meeting of two profoundly American philosophies, the individualist and libertarian frontier and the communitarian and spiritual Quakerism. The Grateful Dead's jams, persecuted by the System, thus actually expressed better than any other musical phenomenon of the time the essence of the American nation, and perhaps for this very reason they 'resonated' so effectively with the souls of thousands of young people. Many young people became hippies and went to concerts by the Grateful Dead.

We have already pointed out that the Grateful Dead were born with San Francisco acid rock, at the same time as the Quicksilver Messenger Service of Dino Valenti, Gary Duncan, David Freiberg and John Cipollina.[7] However, they managed to transform that subcultural idiom

6. To listen to them, cf. http://gratefuldeadprojects.com/Jam_Segments. html. For further information, see http://deadessays.blogspot.it/2010/01/deads-early-thematic-jams.html. For a thoughtful critical analysis, see Malvinni, *Grateful Dead and the Art of Rock Improvisation*, 277.

7. Together with Jerry Garcia, John Cipollina is considered one of the fathers of San Francisco acid rock, who died prematurely in 1989 at only forty-six years of age. He used to play using fingerpicks and making extensive use of the tremolo bridge which, he explained to Jerry Garcia, he needed to remedy the weakness of his left hand. For his part, Jerry Garcia was missing the middle finger of his left hand, which had been accidentally amputated by his brother

into a universal language that transcended the milieu of the hippies and reached almost every corner of the planet.[8] Their psychedelic music was a kind of intellectual muzak that reinterpreted the lysergic 'trip' as a cathartic escape from everyday reality and liberation from urban neuroses. In practice, theirs was a psychological investigation into the relationship between altered states of the mind (psychedelic hallucinations) and altered states of the psyche (the neuroses of industrial society). As already mentioned, their background and original musical technique came from the Acid Test experience of Ken Kesey and the Merry Pranksters, and in those days Jerry Garcia's nickname was 'Captain Trip'.

In the early years of their experience, the Dead played a lot and thus had the opportunity to hone their techniques to the point of becoming excellent blues, country and even jazz musicians, and not just skilled architects of psychedelic 'trip' soundtracks.

In the beginning, the Grateful Dead had thus become the apostles of the orgy, of the collective orgasm, of psychedelic happenings. The Vietnam War and student protests were quite foreign to their musical philosophy, even though they were among its best interpreters. They declared themselves, in fact, mostly apolitical, very self-referential, especially from a musical point of view, in search of a psychomotor well-being independent of any ideology. The Grateful Dead represented rebellious young people who sought physical and mental excitement, not the construction of a better world. Their performances were exhausting and hallucinatory.

At the same time, however, the Dead were part of a family of hundreds, if not thousands, of people, mostly artists, who supported themselves with everyone's income, and who lived on the fringes of the establishment, rejecting its market laws. The Dead were therefore the most Dionysian image of acid rock, but also the symbol of community life.

at the age of four! Quicksilver's most famous record is *Happy Trails* from 1969, considered to be among the best rock records ever.

8. Italy, unfortunately, was a negative exception, so much so that there was never a live performance by them. The first and only concert after the Grateful Dead ended after Jerry Garcia's death in 1995 was the Bob Weir & Ratdog concert at Idroscalo in Milan on 13 July 2002.

Jerry Garcia (born 1942) was a bluegrass guitarist, fascinated by the otherworldly style of fiddler Scotty Stoneman (capable of stretching a bluegrass song to twenty minutes with ever-longer phrases) and the free-jazz of John Coltrane. Garcia met poet and singer Robert Hunter at the college where they were studying in 1960, and together they formed an ensemble that also took part in a local folk festival. Also part of the Palo Alto folk circuit were the Zodiacs of drummer Bill Kreutzmann and pianist Ron Mc Kernan, known as 'Pigpen', who also played rock and roll and blues. From the meeting of the two groups a jug-band was born with Garcia, Pigpen and guitarist Bob 'Weir' Hall (Mother McCree's Uptown Jug Champions). The band's style evolved towards blues and electric rock, while the line-up grew with Kreutzmann and classically trained and jazz-experienced bassist Phil 'Lesh' Chapman (violin prodigy and electronic experimenter). They adopted electric instrumentation, changed their name to Warlocks and performed for the first time in July 1965.

But this name did not last long. When they learned that the same name was also being used by a young New York rock band, which would later become famous as the Velvet Underground, they decided to change it.

This liaison with the Velvet Underground is truly a special case. Never could the two bands be further apart. And never more distant were the two charismatic leaders, Lou Reed and Jerry Garcia. The Velvet Underground emerged from the intellectual-alternative milieu of metropolitan New York, which at the time was going through a lot of culturally innovative turmoil. They created (with Nico) the soundtrack to Andy Warhol's Factory: the Factory, the metaphorical, gloomy place, a far cry from the sunny, joyful image of the Dead's music, where, at the limit, more LSD than heroin circulates. And it is not surprising that there was never any chemistry between the two bands, to the point that Lou Reed and Maureen Tucker (the Velvet drummer) declared, before a concert at the Fillmore West in San Francisco, a few days after a Dead concert, that 'there was no more boring music than that played by the Grateful Dead'.[9] However, there is one thing the two groups have in

9. Cf. http://deadessays.blogspot.it/2010/09/velvets-and-dead.html. 'In 1971 Maureen Tucker called the Dead the most boring band she'd ever heard. Sterling Morrison also loathed them, and despised San Francisco music in general. (But he did make an exception for Quicksilver Messenger Service, saying they sounded great and John Cipollina was a really good guitar player.) Lou Reed also

common: both were milestones in the history of American rock music and counterculture.

When the law banning the use of hallucinogens was enacted in California in October 1966, and Ken Kesey, hounded by the police, was forced to take refuge in Mexico, the Warlocks moved, for a very short time, to Los Angeles to the court of the other lysergic guru Augustus Stanley Owsley (who later became their first sound engineer, before being arrested and sentenced to three years for drug use), before returning to the San Francisco Bay Area and residing in the hippy neighbourhood of Haight Ashbury (at 710 Ashbury Street, as already mentioned), under the new name of the Grateful Dead.[10] The Acid Test era was over and with it the period of anarchic and lysergic experimentation; thus began the period that, in a short time, led them to become the leading and reference group for the emerging counter-cultural community.

Even though they shared their audience, the Grateful Dead paradoxically represented a more radical fringe of the hippy public than the Jefferson Airplane, who were much more politicized in their lyrics, because they worked in support of the Frisco hippy community, especially in support of the activity of the Diggers.[11] So much so that,

had harsh things to say (although he did like the first Moby Grape album; and they were fans of LA bands Buffalo Springfield and the Byrds).' In an exchange with Doug Yule in 1970 (guitarist, member of the Velvet Underground from 1968 to 1973), Lou Reed stated: 'We had vast objections to the whole San Francisco scene. It's just tedious, a lie, and untalented. They can't play and they certainly can't write. The Airplane, the Dead, all of them … Jerry's not a good guitar player. It's a joke, and the Airplane is even worse, if that's possible.' It should be noted, however, that the same scornful judgement was also aimed at Frank Zappa, described as 'the single most untalented person I've heard in my life – he's two-bit, pretentious, academic, and he can't play his way out of anything. He can't play rock & roll.' The Velvets couldn't even stand Jefferson Airplane, to the point of turning down a gig so as not to play on the same night.

10. The new name Grateful Dead was decided by randomly extracting two words from a vocabulary, according to the testimony of Jerry Garcia.

11. Cf. D. McNally, *A Long Strange Trip. The Inside History of Grateful Dead* (New York: Broadway Books, 2002). This is the most comprehensive and ponderous biography of the group, at no less than 684 pages. The title is taken from a famous line from the song 'Trucking', written by Robert Hunter: 'What a long strange trip it's been'.

instead of taking advantage of this, they organized a counter-festival[12] in June 1967 in Monterey with free admission, to make it clear that the official festival was anything but in line with hippy ideals. The Grateful Dead not only lived inside the San Francisco counterculture, they were its main direct spokesmen.

For this very reason, perhaps, their recording history is inversely proportional to their rising fame. Besides being the last rock band in San Francisco to sign a contract with a major record company (Warner Bros.), more than a year after the signings of Jefferson Airplane (RCA) and Quicksilver Messenger Service (Capitol), their debut album, *Grateful Dead*, released in the summer of 1967 when all the masterpieces of psychedelia (Doors, Jefferson Airplane, Jimi Hendrix, Velvet Underground, Pink Floyd, Beatles[13]) had already been released, is a sort of compromise with the record industry: instead of offering the jams for which they were becoming a living legend, instead of documenting the unique and revolutionary phenomenon of their concerts, that album presented a traditional repertoire with a sound that was far inferior to their live performances.

The only tracks that hint at the atmosphere of the live performances outside the studios are 'Morning Dew' (which would become a classic of their concerts until the band's break-up in 1995) and 'Viola Lee Blues' (a thirteen-minute crescendo ride on a blues base, reminiscent of Pink Floyd's 'Astronomy Domine' in *Ummagumma*): neither are original songs, but covers of blues classics, revisited, however, in a more electric and distorted key, with a minimum of collective improvisation. The result of the record was very disappointing, displeasing everyone, both the fans and the band members themselves.

In the second half of 1967, the Dead took part in the North West Great Tour, during which time they came into contact with percussionist Mickey Hart and electronic keyboardist Tom Constanten, a friend

12. The young Jimi Hendrix also participated in this counter-festival, according to testimonies, and jammed with the Grateful Dead themselves. Unfortunately, no recordings exist of this experience.

13. We refer, in chronological order, to *The Doors* by The Doors (January 1967), *Surrealistic Pillow* by Jefferson Airplane (February 1967), *Velvet Underground with Nico* by The Velvet Underground (March 1967), *Sgt Pepper Lonely Hearts Club Band* by The Beatles (May 1967), *Are You Experienced* by Jimi Hendrix (May 1967) and *The Piper at the Gates of Dawn* by Pink Floyd (August 1967).

of Lesh's (the band's bass player), who joined the group permanently. Mickey Hart, born in New York, was a child of the art and had started playing drums at an early age. His father, who would later become Reverend Hart, a rather peculiar character whose less than exemplary conduct affected the life of the group,[14] and had won an award for best drummer in the 1950s. The meeting was organized by Bill Kreutzmann, the Dead's only drummer at the time, who invited him to join the band for an evening at the Matrix in San Francisco in late September 1967. After two hours of non-stop improvisation, the Grateful Dead had a second drummer.[15]

Tom Constanten, on the other hand, had studied music, first with composer Luciano Berio when attending Mills College in Oakland, San Francisco (where he had met Lesh) and then in Darmstadt with Karlheinz Stockhausen: a more than unique background, superior even to that of Frank Zappa. Hart was a phenomenon on percussion, not so much for virtuosity but for imagination. Hart's and Constanten's entry marked a decisive turning point in the group's style, allowing them to attempt the impossible: to translate the atmosphere of the jams performed during Acid Tests onto the record.

The result was *Anthem of the Sun*, again for Warner Bros., released in July 1968, one of the masterpieces of acid rock. Despite the fame of the Grateful Dead's live concerts, the album was painstakingly polished in the studio using all sorts of effects and techniques.[16]

14. In the 1970s, Mickey Hart's father managed the band's finances from live shows. In 1971, he ran away with the cash to finance his mystical activities and this led Mickey himself to decide to temporarily leave the band. Despite the resulting financial collapse, the Dead took it philosophically (as was their spirit), to the point of writing an ironic song about it: 'He's Gone!'.

15. Cf. McNally, *A Long Strange Trip*, 222–3.

16. In this regard, an amusing anecdote circulates. During the recording of the song 'Born Cross- Eyed', Bob Weir told Warner Bros. sound engineer Dave Hassinger, who was considered to be one of the best, that it was necessary to reproduce a 'thick air' type sound. The request completely displaced Hassinger, who, putting his hands in his hair, declared that he was no longer able to meet the band members' extravagant demands! Cf. McNally, *A Long Strange Trip*, 233. An account of the fact, by Robert Hunter, can be found in the DVD, *Anthem to Beauty*, which recounts the genesis of the two psychedelic albums, *Anthem of the Sun* and *Aoxomoxoa*.

The band members were inspired by the electronic music of Karlheinz Stockhausen, the 'prepared' instruments of John Cage, and the tape music of Morton Subotnick. The blues and country roots of the band were distorted by violent hallucinogenic shocks. The songs expanded out of proportion, disintegrating the structure of the song, and each piece became a huge bedlam of rhythms, melodies and improvisations in which rock, jazz and the avant-garde blend. The entire instrumentation is used in an innovative way: percussion beats obsessive and multiform to reproduce lysergic pulsations; electronic effects color the nightmares and ecstasy of the psychedelic journey with strong colors; dark and mysterious keyboards chase with a continuous catacomb-like wail; guitars sting and delirious; voices float, soft and depraved. And the instrumentation is much expanded from the traditional rock band set-up, with harpsichord, trumpet, timpani, gongs, bells, prepared piano, celeste, tape. The sound is complex, dense and mellow, overflowing with lines and sounds, careful to fuse and expand the thematic chameleonism of Zappa, the harmonic experimentalism of Pink Floyd, the instrumental improvisation of Cream and the cosmic existentialism of Sun Ra.[17]

The album's best known piece is the long suite 'That's It for the Other One',[18] which contains lyrics praising Neal Cassidy and Acid Tests, and is divided into four parts: the soft country ballad 'Cryptical Envelopment', the pounding and chaotic blues-rock jam 'Quadlibet for Tender Feet', the reprise of the initial leitmotif 'The Faster We Go' and the spectral and lugubrious 'We Leave the Castle', with lots of chains, bells, squeaks and mutes. The recording methods are completely innovative. In fact, producer Dave Hassinger overdubbed several renditions of the piece to achieve a 'multi-dimensional' effect, producing a full, precise sound that improved on Phil Spector's recording techniques with the 'wall of sound', a term that the Grateful Dead later revived in the early 1970s for live recordings. The Dead are the first to make such explicit recourse to noise: thanks to Hart and Kreuzmann's multiple percussion instruments and Constanten's surreal fantasy, they serve to create an oppressive sense of anguish, but at the same time of liberation (as can be seen in the

17. Cf. http://www.scaruffi.com/vol2/grateful.html.
18. The piece would become a Dead classic with the shortened title 'The Other One'. The name derives from a line by Weir (the main songwriter), who once said, referring to the jam: 'This is then the other one' – typical Dead spirit!

drum solo that marks the transition from 'Cryptical Envelopment' to the following track). Pigpen's organ, a cross between the 'gospel' church organ and Al Kooper's 'bass' folk-rock organ, repeats traditional blues turns in an almost obsessive manner, lending musicality to the whole. The Dead also coined a rock music hinged on two rhythms not always in consonance: Hart and Kreuzmann did not just play two different percussive instruments, they played in two almost diametrically opposed styles.

But it is difficult to define a single identity to the tracks. 'New Potato Caboose' begins with a soft, liquid jazz atmosphere, punctuated by the tinkles of Pigpen's vibraphone and the gentle chiming of guitars, swells with a lysergic solo by Garcia and explodes in the final duet of modal guitar and jazz organ.

Lesh's classical background inspires the quarter-hour chamber piece 'Alligator': after a muddled, Goliardic country introduction, with gospel harmonies and a vernacular trumpet, African percussion and distorted vocals provide the sonic basis for a boisterous ritual dance that leads to a state of collective hypnosis, where Garcia's guitar distortions rage. The organ drags all the instruments to the peak of their 'thunderousness' in a rambling jam.

The Dead are masters at playing in a state of musical rarefaction where rhythm and melody no longer exist, but only psychophysical excitement, under the banner of tribal dance and wild primitivism. 'Caution' (the first versions of which date back to the days of Acid Text from the end of 1965) relies on an organ crescendo that soon bursts into a concert of excruciating dissonances, with Constanten's electronics in full evidence. Here, too, shrieks, dilated sounds, hisses, silences, drops, animalistic verses, erase the last traces of music and sink inanimate into the subconscious.

Anthem of the Sun is definitely a milestone of psychedelic rock and reaches heights that will be unsurpassed. It provides emotions that are very different from what Jimi Hendrix's space guitar can offer. If the latter, like no one else, is able with a single instrument to create atmospheres and excitement as if the musicians were a far greater number, the Dead, using as many as ten instruments, manage to recreate a far more sophisticated but equally exciting musical whole.

The technique with which the songs are constructed is always the same: they begin by taking their cue from the roots of American music (country or blues), that is, starting from popular reality, from life outside, in the open air (and the reference to the Sun is not entirely coincidental), and arrive at an improvised delirium over which the guitar soars and under which the organ bellow, often bordering on totally dissonant and percussive chaos; that is, they arrive at the inner life. Everything is then spiced up by Jerry Garcia's guitar improvisations: from the apparent cosmic chaos, almost magically one arrives at an almost delicate and harmonic warp.

The Dead's traditional acid-rock roots are most evident in *Aoxomoxoa* (Warner Bros., June 1969). Here, the cosmic and seemingly haphazard sound of *Anthem of the Sun* is structured according to a form closer to the ballad: country and blues blend seamlessly with psychedelia, while the percussion rediscovers the orthodox meaning of the word 'rhythm'.

Almost all the tracks follow a similar, less anarchic cliché, albeit with eccentric arrangements, but on a traditional basis, with shrewd but valuable exploitation of the instrumentation, so much so that at certain moments it sounds like listening to Robertson's Band. Emblematic in this regard is the song 'St. Stephen', which will come to play an important role in the symbolic imagery, taking up the image of the *rose* (already present in 'That Is for the Other One'), which together with the *skull*, will become the iconography of the group. In this track, the Dead alternate between a powerful and syncopated gospel-rock, a lysergic lullaby and again the inflamed grit of a boogie. 'Dupree's Diamond Blues' harkens back to 1920s orchestras and street organs, to vaudeville ragtime (complete with banjo). So does 'Doin' That Rag', with abrupt tempo changes and a passionate crooner tone.[19] 'Rosemary' is even a serenade but with the voice distorted by a filter. These are very formal songs without equal in the Bay Area, adapting two centuries of American (mostly black) music to the spirit of the hippies.

Elsewhere, however, the harmonic games become more complex and estranging. 'Mountains of the Moon' is a kind of light ballad, characterized by a harmonic melody. Equally innovative and peculiar are the harmonic juxtapositions of 'China Cat Sunflower' (with Robert Hunter's lysergic lyrics), with a beach accordion, a surf choir, a gospel dirge, with a bluesy guitar counterpoint. Typical of the 'dilated' style with which classic genres are reinvented, 'Cosmic Charlie' drifts along with

---

19. The crooner style originated in the United States, after the advent of the microphone. Tradition dictated that the singer's voice was stentorian and loud, so that it could clearly reach the back rows of the theatres; the use of the microphone makes vocal power less indispensable and allows the singer to use a whispering technique. Crooning is thus not a specific musical genre, but rather a style. Cf. https://en.wikipedia.org/wiki/Crooner.

a lazy, 'lived-in' blues, in the background a splendid 'Hawaiian' chirp from Garcia and Lesh's bass counterpoint. Different and innovative is 'What's Become of the Baby', a litany that chants the Tibetan music of the Hare Krishna mantra.

On the whole, *Aoxomoxoa* thins out the improvisation but condenses the energy, and its synthesis work definitively fixes acid rock. Tracks like 'Mountains of the Moon' place them among the greatest arrangers of the time, beyond their party affiliation.

But we repeat: the group's natural element was live performances, during which the Grateful Dead became the psychedelic equivalent of a chamber quintet or a free-jazz combo and played oceanic versions of their classics. At the end of 1969, recordings of some of these memorable performances were released on a double album entitled *LiveDead* (Warner Bros., November 1969), which we have already mentioned. The atmosphere is electric and exhilarating, the tracks are endless and the sunny climate urges sensual, soft vibrations; each track is a progression that could go on forever, a snake of sound cells that blaze intermittently, a coitus interruptus replicated without end.

If 'The Eleven' is Garcia's unpredictable guitar and 'Death Don't Have No Mercy' is a gospel that is pure psychedelic entertainment, 'Feedback', 'Turn On Your Love Light' and 'Dark Star' represent 1960s psychedelia. In particular, 'Turn On Your Love Light' represents the triumph of Ron 'Pigpen' McKernan, who was able to bring out his blues soul, and who in live versions with partner Janis Joplin was the protagonist of respectable live performances.[20]

'Feedback' is one long, excruciating guitar twang. It is the most daring experiment Garcia attempted in his career as a guitarist; a dissonant guitar sonata, constructed, as the title suggests, using only guitar feedback. It is eight minutes of guitar distortions bordering on noise. It is a daring experiment and not an easy listen, a close relative of the Pink Floyd of 'Interstellar Overdrive' or the Jimi Hendrix of 'Third Stone from the Sun'.

As spectacular and revolutionary as they are, these tracks disappear before the twenty-three minutes of 'Dark Star', the Grateful Dead's masterpiece and the iconic piece of all-time rock psychedelia, in which they sublimate all their techniques to instruments and collective

20. See, for example, the live performance at the Euphoria Ballroom in San Raphael, California on 1 July 1970. Here is the recording of the concert: https://archive.org/details/gd70-07-16.sbd.clugston.6485.sbeok.shnf.

improvisation. The song, composed in 1967, was released in 1968, on the three-minute single 'Dark Star', and is the terminal 'trip' of the Grateful Dead and of all acid rock. Essential and penetrating, the music sways between sweetness and mystery, now soft, now shaggy, clear and murky, terrestrial and cosmic, outer and inner. Visions and delusions, a muted solo and a concert of dissonances, a discontinuous flow of sound. Music to be listened to under the effect of substances to grasp its magic; 'Dark Star', written by Robert Hunter, was born on a winter afternoon in 1967, in San Francisco's Golden Gate Park.[21] It is the last

21. It is worth recalling the genesis of the piece, one of the all-time music classics. In August 1967, Robert Hunter was in Mexico, as was the custom among hippies at the time. He received a communication from Jerry Garcia. The Dead were working on the music of *Alligator* and there was a guitar riff he absolutely had to hear to make a new song. Hunter set out, but because he had no money and was often high on meth (i.e. methamphetamine) it took him about a month to get to Frisco. Phil Lesh picked him up in his car and drove him to Rio Nido (a suburb of San Francisco), where the Dead were busy doing a series of gigs/performances. Garcia played him the guitar riff and Hunter began to think up the lyrics. A few days later, sitting on a bench in San Francisco's Golden Gate Park, with an open notebook on his lap on which he was writing possible verses, he was approached by a hippy who handed him a joint and said, 'Maybe this will help'. Hunter replied, 'Thanks a lot, kid'. And the boy replied: 'In case it helps, this joint is called Dark Star'. Hunter started to smoke it but part of it fell to ashes. Hunter was thinking of T.S. Eliot's poem 'The Love Song of J. Alfred Prufrock' and in particular the line 'Shall we go, then you and I'. Here are the lyrics of the song:

Dark star crashes
Pouring its light into ashes.
Reason tatters
The forces tear loose from the axis.
Searchlight casting
For faults in the clouds of delusion.

Shall we go, you and I, while we can?
Through the transitive nightfall of diamonds.

Mirror shatters
In formless reflections of matter.
Glass hand dissolving

great psychedelic fresco of Jerry Garcia, who became the Bay Area's most legendary guitarist.

The era of acid-testing, consciousness-expanding, happening concerts ended with the 1960s. The unravelling of the Bay Area also involved Garcia and his comrades, who, even more than the others, precisely because they were 'insiders' to what today would be called the 'subjectivity' of the moment, felt the need to breathe different air in order to detoxify themselves of the intoxicating fumes of the past.

Already from the early 1970s, as if to mark a historical caesura, which in Europe would occur in the middle of the decade and in Italy after the 1970s, a period of reflux began. An ebb that was seen as a kind of betrayal by the more hardcore fans, who had seen in the Dead above all the singers of a great sonic chaos. The early senility of the drug addicts and the general climate of reflux heightened the feeling that the Grateful Dead had, for better or worse, marked the contradictory experience of the hippies.

Thus, in 1970, a historic turn in the country took place. Constanten, the main proponent of exoticism and electronics, left the band to follow

To ice petal flowers revolving.
Lady in velvet
Recedes in the nights of goodbye.
Shall we go, you and I, while we can?
Through the transitive nightfall of diamonds.

It is perhaps the most psychedelic lyric ever written, where all the imaginary philosophy of the time and today is present. It is a short lyric for a 23-minute piece of music, but to this day it is still the quintessential unsurpassed psychedelia. The best version of 'Dark Star' is perhaps the one on the *Live Dead* album, taken from the concert at the Fillmore West on 27 February 1969. Deadheads' favourite version is perhaps the over 31' version played at the Old Renaissance Faire in Veneta, Oregon (USA), on 2 August 1972: https://archive. org/details/gd72-08-27.sbd.orf.3328.sbeok.shnf. There have been much longer live versions such as the 43' 27" version on 6 December 1973 at the Public Hall in Cleveland, Ohio (https://archive.org/details/gd73-12-06.sbd.kaplan-fink-hamilton.4452.sbeok.shnf) or the over one hour long, but very spurious 1968 version interspersed with *The Eleven* and credited, however, to Mickey and the Hartbeats (because the Grateful Dead name was already under contract to another venue): https://archive.org/details/gd68-12-16.sbd.hartbeats.4529. sbeok.shnf. Finally, as a final summation, it is essential to listen to *Grayfolded*

his classical vocation: for the record, he would abandon the rock scene altogether, devoting himself to off-Broadway shows and chamber compositions (piano solo and string quartet). Garcia, having freed himself of his destabilizing mind, picks up the twelve-string, slide guitar (the first rock musician to do so), takes off his holy man's tunic and puts on his cowboy hat. The eccentric arrangements disappear altogether and suddenly the sound becomes resigned and crystalline, a move away from the reboant and anarchic.

Workingman's Dead (Warner Bros., 1970) is even an album in the vein of Bakersfield country,[22] particularly reminiscent of Buck Owens[23] and Merle Haggard. This collection of sweet country ballads proceeds at great strides along the involutional line drawn by *Aoxomoxoa*, putting away the hallucinogenic instruments and sharpening (figuratively) the banjos and mandolins. Garcia and Hunter's compositional prowess nonetheless produces a great result: the record's eight tracks, all original, could be as many Nashville (or, rather, Bakersfield) standards. It is a very strong change of direction, but a red thread of psychedelia remains, albeit a well hidden one.

Witness the initial 'Uncle John's Band', mixing vocal and guitar harmonies that are typically Californian, those that Crosby, Stills and Nash were bringing back into vogue in Los Angeles, with the possibility, however, of developing improvisational jams, as happens in the live versions, with nuances reminiscent of the psychedelic harmonies of 'St. Stephen'. Behind tracks such as 'High Time' and 'Black Peter', the structure of long acid-rock pieces can be sensed, but instead of lysergic sabbaths, Garcia's voice and guitar prefer to stretch out in calm, relaxed, 'stornellate', imperceptible syncopations. 'Dire Wolf', 'Cumberland Blues' (modelled on Buck Owens's 'Working Man Blues') are canonical in that acoustic and choral dimension, perfect appendages to centuries of old-time music in keeping with all the

(1994), the two-CD album produced by John Oswald featuring new edits and re-mixes of the Grateful Dead song 'Dark Star'.

22. The Bakersfield sound is a genre of country music that developed in the second half of the 1950s around Bakersfield, California. John Dawson, co-founder of the New Riders of the Purple Sage and great friend of Jerry Garcia, and in the 1970s a constant presence in the Grateful Dead's live shows, is one of the best-known performers.

23. Owens's guitarist Don Rich had been a major influence on Garcia, particularly that way of starting a song on the 'wrong' chord.

stereotypes of the style (bluegrass pulse, vocal harmonies, intertwining of stringed instruments). The most sinister atmospheres, mindful of the psychedelia of yesteryear, are found in the swamp-rhythm gospel of 'New Speedway Boogie' and the voodoo dance of 'Easy Wind'. But the classic that seals the record is 'Casey Jones', with its peculiar lyrics and crescendo music that perhaps best sanctions the definitive transition from psychedelia to country.

The following album, released not even six months later (a testament to the band's creative vein at the time), with the indicative title *American Beauty*, is even more acoustic and uncluttered, marking a greater departure from the 1960s. 'Trucking' and 'Sugar Magnolia', representing post-acid songs respectively, are the classics that the Dead add to their repertoire.

The crisis within the line-up began with the departure of Mickey Hart in 1971 (he would return four years later with a wealth of nascent world music). Garcia for his part played with Paul Kantner and Grace Slick and the newly formed New Riders of the Purple Sage.

Jerry Garcia's solo album, *Garcia* (Warner Bros., 1972), where in fact all the band members play, is more innovative than *American Beauty*. The album is a kind of bridge, or rather passage, from psychedelic civilization to country-rock roots, but mediated by the unbridled experimentalism of art rock. The album is in fact made up of two distinct parts: a country side (with two superb signature ballads, 'Deal' and the mournful 'Loser', with a skilful use of steel guitar by Garcia) and an electronic side. The latter is a single concert that begins with the dissonances of 'Spider Gowd' and continues with the piano sonata of 'Eep Hour', quilted with a melodic phrase repeated first by the synth and then by the steel guitar in a psychedelic crescendo, and culminating in the almost Jeffersonian epic of 'The Wheel'.

Weir (who in the meantime had greatly increased his guitar skills) also recorded a solo album, *Ace*, in 1972 (which saw, as usual, the involvement of all band members). This album featured songs that the Dead already played live, such as 'Black-Throated Wind', 'Playing in the Band', 'Looks Like Rain' and the aforementioned 'Cassidy', which would become classics, mostly written by John Perry Barlow, who had joined Robert Hunter in writing the lyrics.

In March 1973, Pigpen died, having been ill for months and no longer in tune with the band's country turn. Pigpen, with Garcia, had in fact been the true inspiration of acid rock and a great fan of the blues: he would be replaced by Keith Godchaux, who would leave the band in 1979 and who would shortly afterwards also die in a car accident. In his place would sit Brent Mydland, who would also die in 1990 from an overdose, thus confirming the grim fate of the band's keyboardists.

In the early years of the decade, the Grateful Dead only produced live records, the best of which is the first *Dead Live* of 1971, with a suite, 'The Other One', which is the swan song of acid rock and Pigpen. *Live* contains one of their best ballads, 'Wharf Rat'. The album, best known among Deadheads as *Skull and Roses* because of the cover image, designed by Alton Kelly and Stanley Mouse, should have been called *Skull Fuck* according to the band's wishes, a name rejected by Warner Bros.

The triple *Europe 72* (Warner Bros., 1972) bears witness to the band's first structured European tour and is an opportunity to do a kind of career summary. Musically, more interesting is *Hundred Year Hall* (Grateful Dead Records), released posthumously, which contains material from the concerts themselves, including a 36-minute 'Cryptical Envelopment'.

In 1973, to better control their musical production and distribution and not be subject to the impositions of the majors (as had been the case with *Dead Live*), the group decided to found their own record company, Grateful Dead Records, proving to be pioneers of self-organization in this field as well. However, the experiment was not as successful as they had hoped, not least because of the financial difficulties of those years, and the label was closed in 1977, although it occasionally reopened for the release of live repertoire material.[24]

However, when audiences discovered their natural predisposition for excitement and good vibes, the band suddenly became an international attraction. They held vast gigs all over the place (600,000 people at Watkins Glens in 1973,[25] and even an evening in the pyramids of Egypt in 1978[26]) and began to climb the sales charts, without ever breaking into the top ten (which would only happen with the new studio album after seven years of silence, in 1987: *In the Dark*). In short order, the Dead came to contend with Pink Floyd (with whom they rivalled for a long time in the size of the PA system) for the reputation of the greatest show in rock history.

The new course with their own publishing house began with the release of *Wake of the Flood* (1973), where we find an elegant sound,

24. Cf. *Dick's Pick* series.
25. Cf. https://archive.org/details/gd1973-07-28.aud.weiner.106793.flac24.
26. Cf. https://archive.org/details/gd1978-09-16.gems.BEAR.108845.flac24.

but one that is now sustained by the always remarkable craftsmanship and painstaking production work. It is the beginning of a period of creative crisis, which not coincidentally coincides with the crisis of the social movements that had swept through the previous decade. The music stays in the groove of two strands: rock songs, which often lack the innovative, counter-cultural and alternative skills of the old days, and soft jazz-orchestral suites. To the first strand belong 'Eyes Of The World', 'Stella Blue' and 'Mississippi Half-Step Uptown Toodleoo' from *Wake of the Flood*; 'China Doll', 'Unbroken Chain' and 'Pride Of Cucamonga' from *From the Mars Hotel* (1974); 'The Music Never Stopped' and 'Franklin's Tower' from *Blues for Allah* (1975); 'Passenger' from *Terrapin Station* (1977); 'Shakedown Street', 'Fire On The Mountain', 'I Need A Miracle' and 'If I Had The World to Give' from *Shakedown Street* (1978); 'Alabama Gateway' from *Go to Heaven* (1980). The second strand, however superior, includes 'Weather Report Suite' from *Wake of the Flood*, with a fascinating prelude reminiscent of a piece of classical music; *Blues for Allah* (1975); *Terrapin Station* (1977), with orchestration by Paul Buckmaster; 'Drums/Space', one of their live rituals; and 'Althea' (1979). It was a period of fatigue, enlivened by some legendary live concerts such as the four nights at the Winterland in San Francisco in 1977 or the New Year's Eve concert on 31 December 1978, also at the Winterland in San Francisco, certainly one of the best and most famous rock concerts of that period.[27]

27. It was the closing of the Winterland, a historic venue in San Francisco. The evening, according to those present, was unforgettable. It began at 6 p.m. with a preview of John Landis's just-released film *Animal House* starring John Belushi, followed by a concert by The Blues Brothers (with Belushi himself and Dan Aykroyd) and a set by the New Riders of Purple Sage. At midnight, the Grateful Dead took the stage, who, after the midnight countdown (with the voice of actor Dan Aykroyd), began with 'Sugar Magnolia'. The concert lasted almost five hours (net of breaks, 4 hours 22 minutes), one of the longest live concerts in the history of rock music. At 6 a.m., as announced on the poster, breakfast was served ('breakfast served at dawn'). After more than 1,000 days in San Francisco, 'Dark Star' was played, in a medley with 'The Other One', lasting about 35 minutes. The set list of the concert can be found here: http://www.setlists.net/?show_id=1133. The concert, like others by the Grateful Dead, was broadcast free of charge by San Francisco's public radio station KPFM to allow wider distribution. It is now available in a box set of four CDs and a double DVD, entitled *The Closing of Winterland*. At the concert, almost marking an era,

However, the era was coming to an end. It was no coincidence that the decade was consecrated by two live performances, *Dead Set* and *Reckoning*, both released in 1981 and recorded, for the most part, at Radio City Music Hall in New York, the former electric to recall the days of psychedelia, the latter entirely acoustic, to recall the days of country.

We have to wait until 1987 for a new Grateful Dead record. Meanwhile, bootlegs go crazy. The epic and nostalgic country-rock of 'Hell in a Bucket' (written by Weir), 'West L.A. Fadeaway', 'Black Muddy River', 'Throwing Stones' (about the dangers of nuclear power plants) and above all 'Touch of Grey' make up the new album, *In the Dark*. Paradoxically, with this album will also come chart success. For the first time in their career, the single 'Touch of Grey' enters the top ten of the American charts and will give the Dead their first platinum record. It is the first studio album in seven years, due to Garcia's poor health and his drug addiction.

The following album in 1989, *Built to Last* (Arista, 1989) is, without infamy or praise, mostly composed by keyboardist Brent Mydland. However, Garcia penned 'Standing on the Moon' and Weir continued his personal saga with 'Victim or the Crime' (perhaps his masterpiece). Once again the decade would be sealed by a monumental live album, *Without a Net* (Arista, 1990).

Like a pearl in the firmament and as a final epitaph, *Infrared Roses* (Grateful Dead Records) appeared in 1992. It is a collection of instrumental jams, one of their most eccentric and least known records, but of great artistic and musical value, the only one that links up with *Anthem of the Sun*.

Jerry Garcia died on 9 August 1995 of cardiac arrest while in a drug rehabilitation centre. He was fifty-three years old.

Here the musical history of the Grateful Dead ends. The name, in memory of the late Jerry Garcia, will no longer be used and this alone tells us of the band's rigour and consistency. The band members will continue with solo or partly group experiments, always at a respectable

John Cipollina of the Quicksilver Messenger Service also played and Ken Kesey spoke. The recording of the entire concert is available here: https://archive.org/details/gd1978-12-31.fob.akgd224e.holwein.motb-0130.106102.flac16. As of 15 January 2015, the entire concert, with interviews and breaks, can also be viewed and listened to on YouTube in a 5h 47' 27" long film: https://www.youtube.com/watch?v=yKzrZENiERU.

musical level, under different names: Ratdog, The Other Ones and now Further.

Garcia's death triggers an avalanche of memorial publications. Phil Lesh edited a collection of unreleased live tracks recorded between 1967 and 1995, *Fallout from the Phil Zone* (Grateful Dead, 1997) including a half-hour version of Wilson Picket's classic 'In the Midnight Hour' (recorded in 1967).

The year 1999 saw the release of *So Many Roads* (Arista, 1999), a five-CD, live box set containing some of the band's best jams (from *Soundcheck Jam* to *Beautiful Jam*).

Finally, in the writer's opinion, it is worth mentioning *Grayfolded*: a studio album by the Grateful Dead and John Oswald, originally released in 1994 under the title *Grayfolded: Transitive Axis* and reissued in 1996 on a double CD with added tracks. The album was released when Grateful Dead bassist Phil Lesh invited Oswald to assemble more than one hundred different recordings of live performances of 'Dark Star' into one very long version. After gaining access to the archives of the band's recordings, Oswald spent several months combining the numerous tapes together using digital equipment. After being released on a single CD, the album material was expanded with a 'second part' named 'Mirror Ashe'. Given that 'Dark Star' is the emblem not only of the Grateful Dead but of a certain psychedelic way of experiencing rock music (and we might add, life) that has influenced and still influences, even if not consciously, contemporary life, with all its contradictions, this work thirty years after the group's birth seals its immortality.

In 2015, fifty years after the birth of the Grateful Dead, five concerts are held, in which the band members reunite for the first and last time since Jerry Garcia's death. The event is called 'Fare Thee Well: Celebrating 50 Years of the Grateful Dead'. The shows were performed on 27 and 28 June at Levi's Stadium in Santa Clara, California, and on 3, 4 and 5 July at Soldier Field in Chicago, Illinois, where the Grateful Dead's last concert before Jerry Garcia's death twenty years earlier had taken place on 9 July 1995 in front of almost 100,000 spectators.[28]

The line-up consisted of the 'four cores', Bob Weir, Phil Lesh, Micky Hart and Bill Kreutzmann, with the addition of Phish's Trey Anastasio on guitar (with the burden and honour of replacing Jerry Garcia), Jeff Chimenti on keyboards, and Bruce Hornsby on piano. All concerts sold

---

28. Here is a recording of the concert: https://archive.org/details/gd95-07-09.sbd.7233.sbeok.shnf.

out and were recorded by many media outlets as well as being freely live, as was in the spirit of the Grateful Dead. The Chicago shows are scheduled to be released as a CD and DVD box set.

President Obama wrote:

> Here's to fifty years of the Grateful Dead, an iconic American band that embodies the creativity, passion, and ability to bring people together that makes American music so great. Enjoy this weekend's celebration of your fans and legacy. And as Jerry would say, 'Let there be songs to fill the air'.[29]

29. E. Leight, 'President Obama Calls the Grateful Dead an "Iconic American Band" in Touching Tribute', *Billboard*, 5 July 2015.

Chapter 3

EXODUS, COMMUNITY SPIRIT AND THE COMMONS

The 1960s saw the birth and spread of hippy culture and philosophy.

The word hippy derives from hipster and was initially used to describe the beatniks who had elected the Haight Ashbury district of San Francisco as a place to live, mainly due to the low cost of rents. The beatniks had inherited the cultural values of the Beat Generation, fostering the birth and spread of a counterculture with its communities that listened to psychedelic rock, embraced the sexual revolution and the use of drugs such as hallucinogens and cannabis to explore and expand the state of consciousness.

The writer Jesse Sheidlower, the leading American editor of the *Oxford English Dictionary*, states that the terms *hipster*, *hippy* or *hippie*[1] derive from the word 'hyp', short for 'hypochondria': the origin lies in their supposed inclination to melancholy and – if we want to translate the slang term better – to their melancholic and 'hypochondriac' aspect in the romantic sense of the term. From a purely etymological point of view, the term hypochondria derives in ancient Greek from the union of two words: *hypo* meaning 'under' and *chondros* meaning 'sternum': literally, *under the sternum*, where, according to Hippocrates' medicine, melancholic affliction was born. In current parlance, hypochondria indicates the pathological state of one who is distressed by illnesses, but its romantic meaning in the nineteenth century rather indicated one who took care of one's health, an aspect that was taken up by the hippy philosophy to the point of

1. On the correct spelling of the two terms: hippy or hippie, there is a lengthy discussion, which we are not interested in resuming here. Let us consider them synonymous, using only the term hippy.

extending it not only to the body but also to the mind, through the increase of cerebral and sensory perceptions (thanks, in fact, to the use of special drugs).

The term *hipster* was coined by Harry Gibson in 1940 and was often used in the 1940s and 1950s to describe jazz performers.[2] Hippy was also slang used in 1940, and one of the earliest recorded uses of the word hippy can be traced to a radio programme aired on 13 November 1945, in which Stan Kenton called Harry Gibson, 'hippie'. However, it seems that when Kenton used the word he meant to make a pun on Gibson's nickname 'Harry the Hipster'. Going back to the Harlem in the late 1940s, Malcolm X recalled in his 1964 autobiography how the term hippy was at that time used by African Americans to describe a certain type of white man, who 'acted more like a black man than the blacks themselves'.

The slang derivation of the hippy is therefore evident. However, it was in the mid-1960s that the term began to be used in print, starting with the article 'A New Haven[3] for Beatniks' by San Francisco journalist Michael Fallon on 5 September 1965. In this article, reference was first made to a new generation of beatniks, who had moved from North Beach to the Haight Ashbury district in San Francisco.[4]

In 2002, photographer-journalist John Bassett McCleary published a 650-page comprehensive slang dictionary (6,000 words), on the language of hippies, entitled *The Hippie Dictionary: A Cultural Encyclopaedia* of the 1960s and 1970s. The book was later revised and expanded to 700 pages in 2004. McCleary believes that the hippy counterculture added a significant number of words to the English language, borrowing from the lexicon of the Beat Generation, shortening words and popularizing their use.

2. http://en.wikipedia.org/wiki/Hippy.

3. It is likely that this title plays on the double meaning in pronunciation between haven (literally 'refuge') and heaven.

4. In this article, Fallon wrote about the Blue Unicorn Café, one of San Francisco's first hippy hangouts, the forerunner of many similar activities, including the Family Dog collective, a community experience that had its origins in the early 1960s and was the forerunner of the first self-produced music, combining the folk music of New York's Greenwich Village with the emerging psychedelic music. The Family Dog also organized the first noteworthy alternative public event, attended by more than 10,000 people: the Trip Festival during 21–3 January 1966 at Longhersman Hall in San Francisco.

Not only did the hippy movement coin new words, but it also revised in a negative sense many terms that in the 1960s represented in mainstream thinking the flagship of the American model: technocracy, bureaucracy, organizational efficiency, multinationals, the machine, the system, the consumer society, up to the very concept of capitalism. Mario Savio's speech at the University of Berkeley,[5] one of the centres of learning of the future elite of the military-industrial apparatus, shows us how the generation of the 1960s was capable of being the bearer of a new culture and not simply a 'subculture', as the hobos, the hipsters of the 1930s and 1940s, had been considered until then.

After the Second World War, new managerial and sociological literature developed that described the characteristics of American Fordism, sometimes in a critical sense but more often in an accommodating sense. Think of Adolf Berle and Gardiner Means's *The Modern Corporation and Private Property* (1932), James Burnham's *Managerial Revolution* (1941), Peter Drucker's *The Concept of the Corporation* (1946), William H. Whyte's *The Organisation Man* (1956), David Riesman's *The Lonely Crowd* (1950), C. Wright Mills's *White Collar: The American Middle Classes* (1951) and *The Power Elite* (1956).[6]

5. See Chapter 1.

6. In his famous farewell address to the nation on 17 January 1961, President Eisenhower himself recognized the existence of the close connection between the power structure and war and the military structure as a condition for future progress but also as a possible danger and therefore called for greater transparency. On this occasion, the term *military-industrial complex* was coined and publicly circulated for the first time:

> A vital element in peacekeeping are our military institutions. Our weapons must be powerful, ready for instantaneous action, so that no potential aggressor can be tempted to risk his own destruction ... This conjunction of an immense body of military institutions and a huge arms industry is new in the American experience. Total influence in the economy, in politics, even in spirituality; it is felt in every city, in every state body, in every office of the federal government. We recognise the imperative need for this development. But nevertheless, we must not fail to understand its grave implications. Our philosophy and ethics, our resources and our way of life are involved; the backbone of our society. In government councils, we must guard our backs against the acquisition of influences that give no guarantees, whether overt or covert, exercised by the *military-industrial complex.*

It was in many of these texts that the 1960s generation was formed. And it started to criticize them.

If we accept Stuart Hall's definition of culture in the broad sense, in which culture is 'everything that defines the *way of life* of a people, a community, a nation or a social group',[7] the hippy movement was not the initiator of a 'subculture', but of an 'other' culture, a counterculture, as Theodore Roszak stated in his 1968 book, *The Making of a Counter Culture*, first coining the term: 'When members of a group pose their subculture as a whole alternative to the dominant culture in society, then the subculture becomes a counterculture.'[8]

And it is from the cornerstones of the hippy counterculture that we start to better understand our times. Because, even though this is often misunderstood, it is from the set of values and ethics underlying the hippy counterculture that the philosophy of contemporary capitalism, founded on knowledge, finance and individual libertarian anarchy, was born and developed.

The hippy counterculture

The hippy counterculture broke new ground. We are not referring here to musical, theatrical and artistic production or fashion, which in any case marked an epoch, but to the attempt to change behaviour, in the sense of ethics and imagery. We are therefore referring to the attempt to construct a new ethics of life and human relations, which originate from the anti-authoritarian yearning that pervades hippy philosophy.

Libertarian anti-authoritarianism stems, as we have seen, from the refusal to be complicit with the military-industrial apparatus and its disciplinary devices that had characterized post-war American economic growth. It finds its roots in Allen Ginsberg's poem 'Howl', published by Ferlinghetti in 1955, a 'cry' that was not desperate but

See   http://www.eisenhower.archives.gov/all_about_ike/speeches/farew ell_address.pdf.

7. Cf. S. Hall, *Critical Dialogues in Cultural Studies*, edited by D. Morley and K.-H. Chen (New York: Routledge, 1996), 2.

8. Quoted in O. Fraysse, 'How the US Counterculture Redefined Work for the Age of the Internet', in O. Fraysse and M. O'Neil (eds), *Digital Labour and Prosumer Capitalism: The U.S. Matrix* (London: Palgrave Macmillan, 2015), 30–50.

that praised liberation on all levels: heterosexual, homosexual, female, religious, racial, but also in solidarity with oppressed peoples and ecological respect. A liberation that can be seen in the now unobtainable 'Vagabond' sticker and in shoulder-strap guitars like Bob Dylan's, with phrases like:

> This machine kills fascists, racists, bigots, cold war supporters, overzealous generals, the Ku Klux Klan, corrupt politicians, complacent clergy.

It is the myth of the journey as a cathartic moment of liberation. It is not emigration, but rather – as we shall see – exodus, because very rarely did the hippies occupy the road in search of work, as had been the case with the hobos, bumps or tramps:[9] vagabonds at the time of Woodie Guthrie, then in the 1930s and 1940s. If the hobos gathered out of desperation in jungles (the encampments on the outskirts of American cities; makeshift shelters made of tin cans and cardboard boxes), the hippies gathered and, to the rhythm of the music, danced, sang and used drugs.

In the history of Made-in-USA antagonism – a history that has always existed and is directly connected with the evolution of the country – the hippy movement represents a discontinuity. Its philosophy and its way of understanding political initiative are placed, at least in its beginnings, on two complementary ridges: infidelity and, precisely, exodus. The first presupposes the second.

Unlike the European movements, with notable exceptions (the main ones being the Black Panther Party – about the Afro-American struggle – and that part of the SDS that will give birth to the Weathermen Underground – about the student and white youth struggle), the hippy movement does not place itself on the plane of direct conflict with the authoritarian institutions of power, whatever the institutionalized level. It practices and propagates lifestyles based on the motto, coined by Timothy Leary, 'Turn on, tune in, drop out'. The meaning and interpretation are: 'turn on your mind' (turn on), tune in to the universe (tune in), drop out of time and present space by realizing yourself (drop out). Even though the mainstream vulgate has always dwelt on the term

9. Bruce Springsteen took up this term in 'Born to Run': 'Oh honey, tramps like us. Baby, we were born to run. Come on with me, tramps like us. Baby, we were born to run.'

'drop out', to the point that it has become the way to represent hippies (in the somewhat derogatory sense, i.e. those who passively 'drop out', the 'slackers', the 'neets'), the three actions must be read in their causal connection. The 'switching on of the mind' means becoming aware, of the process of subjectification, a prerequisite for being able to think of an alternative way of life that does not have to be within the existing social structure. Tuning into the universe, the 'tune in' implies seeking a reason for living and socializing outside the disciplinary structures of the asphyxiated American society, a denial of individual freedom and creativity.

The 'drop out' instead indicates the 'exodus', the journey as a cathartic moment of liberation, detachment but at the same time sedimentation of an alternative way of living, outside the stereotypical bourgeois parameters. Often it is a symbolic manifestation,[10] but just as often it is the experimentation of an alternative life in common. It is therefore a constructive, active exodus and not simply a passive one, that is, a simple escape.

These are subjective and collective dynamics, which – as we have already mentioned – are part of the American culture of the frontier.

The existence of vast territorial spaces, destined for possible colonization thanks also to the genocide of indigenous populations, characterized the development of the American capitalist system at least until the last century. Two of the most relevant consequences, among many, are worth mentioning here. On the one hand, throughout the nineteenth century, the American economy enjoyed the benefits of an original accumulation process that seemed to be without end and allowed for the enlargement of both markets and the accumulation base. On the other hand, the moments of crisis in the capitalist

---

10. As in the case of long hair, an acknowledged symbol of hippy transgression: well recounted in the film-musical *Hair*, when one of the protagonists, detained in jail and subjected to the forced cutting of his long blond hair, goes mad to the point of forcing the guards to call in a psychologist who asks him why he cares so much about having long hair. Here is the answer (where a reference is also made, not accidentally, to the Grateful Dead): 'She asks me why I'm just a hairy guy. I'm hairy noon and night. Hair that's a fright. I'm hairy high and low. Don't ask me why. Don't know. It's not for lack of bread. Like the Grateful Dead. Darling. Gimme head with hair. Long beautiful hair. Shining, gleaming, Steaming, flaxen, waxen. Give me down to there hair. Shoulder length or longer.'

valorization process were marked not only by overproduction or falling profits, but also by the expression of a form of resistance and struggle that in Europe, at least until the 1970s, was more or less unrecognized: workers' desertion from the factories, or the rejection of wage labour.

It should be remembered that this American peculiarity had already been observed by Marx in Book I of *Capital*. Chapter XXV, entitled 'The Modern Theory of Colonisation'[11] (not by chance, immediately following the better-known chapter on 'The So-Called Original Accumulation') analyses the development model of colonies characterized by free access to virgin lands. In the United States, the 'frontier' – that is, the presence of a boundless territory to be populated and colonized – offered American workers the truly extraordinary opportunity to make their condition reversible. Despite the flow of money and cheap labour from the European continent, even though the United States experienced the birth of capitalism concurrently with the original accumulation and not ex-post, without the viscous inheritance of traditional modes of production, the capitalist mode of production in the United States found it very difficult to impose itself, and there was systematic disobedience to the laws of the labour market. The figure of the settler, according to Marx, cannot be equated with that of the wage labourer, precisely because he remains a free man, able to exercise individual ownership over both his means of subsistence and his tools of labour.

> The availability of free land means that wage labour remains a wide net, a provisional status, a time-limited episode: no longer a perpetual identity, an irrevocable destiny, a life sentence. The difference is profound and speaks to us of today. The dynamic of the frontier, the American enigma, constitutes a powerful anticipation of contemporary collective behavior. Having exhausted every spatial outlet, in the societies of mature capitalism, however, the cult of mobility returns, the aspiration to escape a definitive condition, the vocation to desert the factory regime. In contrast to what happened in Europe, at the dawn of American industrialism, there were

11. Cf. K. Marx, *Capital. A Critique of Political Economy. Volume I. Book One: The Process of Production of Capital* (1887), ch. XXVII. Available online: https://www.marxists.org/archive/marx/works/1867-c1/.

not peasants reduced to poverty who became workers, but adult labourers who became free farmers.[12]

The myth of the frontier as a constituent element of political action has always been a factor in social mobilization. In one of the first books published in Italy on the protest movement in the USA in the late 1960s,[13] this myth was recalled as a central aspect for understanding the conflictual dynamics of the American student movement. The theme of the 'exodus' as a process of creative liberation traced a mode of action that has always been part of the American political DNA.

It can therefore come as no surprise that this theme is at the heart of the hippy counterculture, indeed it is its essence. One of San Francisco's most influential psychedelic-rock bands – Jefferson Airplane – made it a manifesto in one of the first concept albums in rock music history: 'It's a fresh wind that blows against the Empire,'[14] by Paul Kantner and Grace Slick, signed by the band's new name: Jefferson Starship. Meaning that the airplane is transformed into a spaceship, capable of exploring and colonizing the new worlds of the galaxy, new territories to be inhabited in alternative forms and ways to the old earthly world. The lyrics of the album represent more than political proclamations, they are manifesto of the hippy philosophy: from the denunciation of oppressive conditions to the demand for freedom,[15] to the desire to escape

---

12. Cfr. W. Simonetti, http://simonettiwalter.wordpress.com/. See also P. Virno, *Esercizi di esodo* (Verona: Ombre Corte, 2002). See in English: https://www.generation-online.org/p/fpvirno5.htm.

13. Cf. A. Cavalli and A. Martinelli (eds), *Gli studenti americani dopo Berkeley* (Turin: Einaudi, 1969).

14. The album's line-up includes the finest names of psychedelic rock from the Bay Area. From the members of the former Jefferson Airplane (Jack Casady, Jorma Kaukonen, Joey Covington as well as Paul Kantner and Grace Slick), to the Grateful Dead (Jerry Garcia, Bill Kreutzmann and Mickey Hart), to David Crosby and Graham Nash, to David Freiberg of the legendary Quicksilver Messenger Service and Harvey Brooks of Electric Flag. Few records have enjoyed such joint participation!

15. 'Put your old ladies back into bed. Put your old men into their graves. Cover their ears so they can't hear us sing. Cover their eyes so they can't see us play. Get out of the way. Let the people play. We're gonna get down on you. Come alive all over you. Dancin' down into your town. ... Close your eyes & create the sound. Open your hands & rebuild the ground. ... I'm alive, I am human, I will

elsewhere,[16] to create a new community spirit. And it is this community spirit that fuels the exodus proposal, which has contaminated an entire generation, even in Europe. Not an exodus as an end in itself, but a constructive exodus.

The hippy movement was essentially a 'white' and libertarian movement. It could not address the African-American community. Blacks were the emblem of working-class and exploited labour; they

be alive again. So drop your fuckin' bombs. Burn your demon babies. Rabid lover-feelin' the starch in your grin. Callin' for acid cocaine and grass

And receiving your homemade gin. Push the bottom, pull the switch, cut the beam, c'mon make it march. … Hey Dick, whatever you think of us is totally irrelevant. Both to us now and to you. We are the present. We are the future. You are the past. Pay your dues and get outta the way 'Cause we're not the way you used to be When you were very young. We're something new. We don't quite know what it is or particularly care. We just do it – You gotta do it. Let the music do it, take you there. Do it, do it, do it – gotta do it. Something new, something new, something new, new, new. Open your eyes there's a new world a-comin'. Open your eyes there's a new world today. Open your hearts people are lovin'. Open it all we've come to stay.' ['Mau Mau', words by Paul Kantner, Grace Slick, Joey Covington]

16. 'Hey – rollin' on. We come and go like a comet. We are wanderers. Are you anymore? The land is green and you make it grow. And you gotta let go you know. You gotta let go you know. You gotta let go you know. Or else you stay. Mankind gone from the cage. All the years gone from your age. At first, I was iridescent. Then, I became transparent. Finally, I was absent.' ['Starship', words by Paul Kantner, Grace Slick, Marty Balin, Gary Blackman]

'Have you seen the stars tonight? Would you like to go up on "A" Deck and look at them with me? Have you seen the stars tonight? Would you like to go up for a stroll and keep me company? Do you know. We could go? We are free. Anyplace you can think of we could be. Have you seen the stars tonight? Have you looked at all the family of stars?' ['Have You Seen the Stars Tonite', words by Paul Kantner, David Crosby]

'You know – a starship circlin' in the sky – it ought to be ready by 1990. They'll be building it up in the air even since 1980. People with a clever plan can assume the role of the mighty and Hijack the Starship carry 7000 people past the sun. And our babes'll wander naked thru the cities of the universe. C'mon: free minds, free bodies, free dope, free music. The day is on its way the day is ours.' ['Hijack', words by Paul Kantner, Grace Slick, Marty Balin, Gary Blackman]

were not allowed to feed off the myth of the frontier. Young whites were the descendants of settlers, they had no history of slavery, violence and direct oppression. Their oppression was essentially 'biopolitical' in nature, it had to do with self-determination before liberation from the shackles of colour-line dictatorship. And perhaps because of this, the social relations of capitalist exploitation were not affected. The plan of action moved more in the superstructural sphere than the structural, even though superstructure and structure were already ambiguously declined at the time, Althusserian-style. Marcuse had more appeal than Marx. But it is precisely the ideology of the frontier, its being irreducible and surplus to the disciplinary rules of the labour market, that on the one hand fuelled the libertarian spirit and at the same time allowed the incessant transformation of the capitalist system of production, its being a process of 'creative destruction', as Schumpeter put it.

The experience of the communes

This ambivalence – building 'elsewhere' rather than fighting 'internally' the brutal conditions of subjugation imposed by industrial capitalism – underlies new forms of social experimentation of a communitarian kind. We refer in particular to the experience of the commune, a modern form of TAZ (Temporary Autonomous Zone). The commune phenomenon began to take hold in the late 1960s.

The new communes in America are quite different from the previous communes, which developed between the end of the eighteenth century and the second half of the nineteenth century.

Donata and Grazia Francescato, in a 1975 text, analyse the differences:

> The communities of the 19th century are utopian, that is, they set themselves up by definition as models for the rest of society: their emphasis is on the social. The communities of today … have more limited aims, they have wiped the slate clean of the grandiose visions – imbued with a profound faith in the future – that animated the communities of the past. The traditional concept of 'salvation' has been traded for the more modest one of 'personal growth', religious or political rhetoric has given way to psychological rhetoric.

This new and more limited dimension of today's movement compared to that of the 19th century can also be seen in the physical structure of the communes: those of the 19th century were rather large communities, with hundreds of members of all ages, those of today are groups often limited to a dozen or so members, mostly young or very young.[17]

The women's liberation movement and the nascent ecological movement contribute greatly to the consolidation of this new community season. The institution of the family, in feminist circles, is seen as a space of discrimination, invisibility and daily harassment of women, while the commune is identified as an interesting possible alternative.

Consequently, the hippy communes were created as alternative structures to the classical family dimension and as laboratories in which this could be, in various ways, disarticulated.

Hence one of the original reasons for the valorization of 'promiscuity', also in the wake of readings of the texts of Wilhelm Reich, Jean-Paul Sartre and Simone de Beauvoir, which were particularly in vogue in those years.

During the 1970s, communitarian experiments multiplied; from the spontaneous open houses, ready to host whoever requested it, to the more or less structured 'urban communes', to the rural communes, even more radical experiments, daughters of an explicitly separatist and proto-ecological instance.

Hostility towards the city was an element particularly dear to the hippies, along with the rejection of the system and distrust of technology.

The experience of the communes, beyond their effective capacity to modify and interfere with the traditional way of life and the individualistic ethics typical of American society, poses a series of questions that are more topical today than yesterday: the concept of the commonwealth and the concept of environmental sustainability.

Common life, the commonwealth and the commons

The experience of the communes represents perhaps the first experiment in relational and cognitive capitalism, anticipating modes and forms of organizing life and time that would be structured in a very un-alternative way and with entirely different aims some thirty years later.

17. D. Francescato and G. Francescato, *Famiglie aperte: la comune* (Milan: Feltrinelli, 1975), 43 (my translation).

The communes, in fact, place learning and relational networks at the centre as the basis of the process of producing use-value. These phenomena are by definition social in nature, that is, they involve developing forms of social cooperation. The organization of work in municipalities is horizontal, in teams, not vertical. And the driving force of social cooperation is language, not only spoken and human language, but also and above all the language of gestures and music; theatre, dance and music are one in the life of the communes.

Unlike what will happen from the 1980s onwards with the birth and spread of artificial, codified and structured languages, we are still in a form of social cooperation that is natural and not induced and modulated by computerized communication techniques.

In this regard, some of Marx's remarks come to mind when, in the *Critique of the Gotha Programme*, he wrote:

> Labor is not the source of all wealth. Nature is just as much the source of use values (and it is surely of such that material wealth consists!) as labor, which itself is only the manifestation of a force of nature, human labor power. ... The bourgeois has very good grounds for falsely ascribing supernatural creative power to labor; since precisely from the fact that labor depends on nature it follows that the man who possesses no other property than his labor power must, in all conditions of society and culture, be the slave of other men who have made themselves the owners of the material conditions of labor. He can only work with their permission, hence live only with their permission.[18]

Nature produces use-value just as human labour activity does. It is capitalism that produces exchange value, transforming man's free activity (his concrete labour) into abstract labour-power under his dependence.

This is made possible by two instruments: private property and the monetization of labour (through wages). It follows that in order to overcome the capitalist system of production, using an active exodus (the drop-out), it is necessary to go beyond private property and towards a conception of the remuneration of labour and life according to the

---

18. Cf. K. Marx, *Critique of the Gotha Programme*, Part 1, Marx/Engels Selected Works, Volume 3 (1875), 13–30. Available online: https://www.marxi sts.org/archive/marx/works/1875/gotha/.

principle (again quoting Marx's *Critique of the Gotha Programme*): 'To each according to his needs, by each according to his abilities.'

The overcoming of private property does not mean the transition to public property but to common property. As is well known, this is a point that is highly topical today. Common property means the non-exclusive possession of a good, which implies the inexistence of scarcity and rivalry. Except for so-called personal property, everything that belongs to the commune is for common use, based on an order of priority that is decided and re-decided collectively according to the capacities and needs of each of the members.

This is not the first time this has occurred in history. Community experiences in many African or Latin American territories have been the subject of in-depth studies, and nowadays a current of anarchist anthropology has developed that deals with such experiences.

Without being fully aware of it, the hippy communes recognized the existence of the common as a 'commonwealth', a preparatory factor for the production of common goods with the sole content of use-value. The commonwealth as non-property.

The commonwealth is nothing other than the dialectical relationship between the members of a community, the outcome of the practice of language and subjective, human relationship, the combination of the 'animal that can speak' and the 'political animal'[19] that defines human nature and whose process of valorization can be aimed at self-valorization, that is, a process of 'production of human being for human being' (use-value), without running the risk of being subsumed by a new ownership structure.

Once the ebb of the hippy counterculture began in the mid-1970s and once it had lost its ethical virginity, the experience of the hippy commune lost its non-proprietary collective meaning. This process of subsumption is what gave rise to the new paradigm of cognitive bio-capitalism.

19. According to a famous definition by Aristotle. Paolo Virno writes: 'Animal that has language: verbal discourse, an integral part of our biological constitution, qualifies all sorts of affections and perceptions. Political animal: trans-individual (or, if you prefer, public) character of the human mind, its capacity to interact, cooperate, adapt to the possible and the unexpected.' Cf. P. Virno, 'A Performative Movement', April 2005. Available online: http://repu blicart.net/disc/precariat/virno01_en.htm.

The commonwealth can take different forms depending on the mode of accumulation, whether it is more based on the exploitation of cognitive-formative faculties or relational-cooperative faculties. To a first approximation, we could call the former the cognitive commonwealth, and the latter the re/productive commonwealth.

The commons have nothing to do with the commonwealth: it is simply an expression of the social cooperation that takes place in the general intellect. It is necessary to be clear about this distinction, because the expropriation of the commons goes beyond the dichotomy between private and public property, in the dialectic of which the question of the management and use of the commons between privatization on the one hand and state ownership on the other arises.

From this point of view, the experience of the hippy commune is an expression of the commonwealth (in the singular), an outcome of social cooperation, capable of producing common goods for the community in a context of non-ownership and total autonomy from the capitalist market and its fetishes.

It deals with the creation of a closed but complete (not therefore partial) economic system, where all stages of circulation and production are present. This completeness is made possible because there are still spaces (physical, real and geographical, but also imaginative and philosophical) where it is possible to locate oneself. It means that there is a possible, uncontaminated and pure 'elsewhere'. And since this space can only be the bare and wild space of nature, hippy communes are mostly agricultural communes, whose purpose is to ensure the survival of their members. Within this framework, the hippies were proponents of a pre-modern, anti-industrial utopia, which proposed a return to a communal life where human beings dominated the machines and not vice versa.

We will return to this point later.

Here we would like to point out that this naturalistic spirit created one of the first ecological movements at a time when environmental awareness was not very developed and when the negative impact on the environment induced by the Fordist industrialization process were not yet apparent.

The naturalistic and environmentalist stance is a salient feature of the American counterculture, and in the 1960s it also took on an anti-technological significance. This spirit derives from the rejection of the machinic, exemplified by Taylorist technologies, as an epiphenomenon of the control of human life. In fact, the technology referred to is the rigid, static, bureaucratic and disciplinary technology on which the authoritarianism of the military-industrial and state apparatus is based, a new form of modern religion from which it is necessary to escape, in the name of a new humanism of solidarity and, indeed, communitarianism. A communitarian spirit that finds its expression in the rejection of violence and the fusion with nature.

Marx's well-known words about religion come to mind:

The foundation of irreligious criticism is: Man makes religion, religion does not make man. Religion is, indeed, the self-consciousness and self-esteem of man who has either not yet won through to himself, or has already lost himself again. But man is no abstract being squatting outside the world. Man is the world of man – state, society. This state and this society produce religion, which is an inverted consciousness of the world, because they are an inverted world. ... The struggle against religion is, therefore, indirectly the struggle against that world whose spiritual aroma is religion.[20]

We have already emphasized how the experience of the commune and collective life – separated from the contamination of the commodification of life – anticipates the idea of a possible overcoming of the dichotomy between private and public property.

At the same time, the communitarian living structure bears witness to the commitment to the environment to this day. Interestingly, almost fifty years later, communal experiences of living in full respect for nature are spreading within the ecovillage network.

The ecovillage is, in fact, a type of community based explicitly on environmental sustainability, founded on a number of basic principles, drawn up by the Australian ecologist and agronomist David Holmgren[21] (who is one of its main theorists): voluntariness; reducing the environmental impact of living structures to a minimum through the use of renewable energy and ecological materials; food self-sufficiency based on permaculture or other forms of organic farming.

It is a laboratory for research and experimentation towards alternative lifestyles to the most widespread socio-economic models.

---

20. K. Marx, 'Critique of Hegel's Philosophy of Right', Introduction, February 1843. Available online: https://www.marxists.org/archive/marx/works/1843/critique-hpr/.

21. Cf. D. Holmgren, *Permaculture: Principles and Pathways Beyond Sustainability* (London: Holmgren Design Services, 2002).

The ecovillage tends towards maximum self-sufficiency, compatible with the need to satisfy as much as possible, within itself, every need of its members (work, leisure, self-expression, education, affective needs …). In this sense, the ecovillage is intended to be a sustainable model, economically, socially and ecologically (using renewable energy and appropriate technologies, defending the environment and the local economy …).

These experiences, which are also spreading in Italy,[22] are also called second-generation communes, to underline the common thread that links them to the American counter-culture experience, but also notes their diversity.[23] Rossella Anitori writes:

> Second-generation communes differ from the first in several aspects. They represent in several respects a more advanced stage of communitarian discourse. If the former are above all experiences of contestation, the latter present themselves as 'attempts at proposal'. The oppositional tension is always there, but it has been consolidated: it is a base from which to start and no longer the goal to aim for. In a certain sense, the phylogeny of communitarianism mirrors the ontogeny of man. And the adolescent phase is succeeded by adulthood. The need to establish a new relationship with nature and between people, the need to move from an anthropocentric to an ecocentric perspective becomes the inspirational pivot of many experiences.[24]

These characteristics are not configured as a form of exodus but, rather, as a path of research that tends to contaminate and blend into the surrounding social fabric, not separate, because it becomes a real example that another way of living is possible.

> A new relationship is configured between city and country, which far from being structured solely in economic terms, outlines a new socio-cultural horizon on the rise: Gas stations, ecological workshops and agritourisms proliferate. Sustainable mobility systems are spreading,

22. The Italian Network of Ecological Villages has been active since 2004: https://it.wikipedia.org/wiki/Rete_Italiana_Villaggi_Ecologici.

23. Cf. R. Anitori, *Vite insieme. Dalle comuni agli ecovillaggi* (Rome: DeriveApprodi, 2012).

24. Cf. Anitori, *Vite insieme*, 14.

time banks, new forms of socialising and exchanging favours, and self-managed childcare services are springing up. The ecological demand from the urban classes grows. In the city, the first cohousing, a special form of neighbourhood that provides a series of collective spaces in addition to individual housing, appeared, so as to safeguard both individual privacy and the need for sociability. An experience somewhere between the commonwealth, where what binds all the members is also the sharing of the economy, and the traditional condominium, where everyone is entrenched in their own flat.[25]

These are, however, forms of community life that maintain a political stance against the diktats of the commodity capitalist system that promotes indifference and individualism as guiding values. These are germs of the communal (in the singular) that, unlike in the past, do not want to escape through exodus but rather inseminate society.

* * * * *

The Grateful Dead community expressed this kind of transition from first-generation to second-generation communes well: the Haight-Ashbury experience in San Francisco did not represent the idea of a closed, self-referential commune but an open, inclusive one.

Paradoxically, the period of collective life in Paul High, on Micky Hart's ranch, was more separate and distant from collective and metropolitan life. And it is no coincidence that it was during this period that the Grateful Dead realized the end of collective psychedelic music and placed themselves on the shores of refined country rock, almost as if searching for the origins of American music.

Nevertheless, the idea of community cooperation is part of the Grateful Dead's DNA, a community spirit that not only represents an important first step in the Grateful Dead economics, but will also be transmitted in the following decades when the same community spirit will transform and forage the hacker spirit.

25. Cf. Anitori, *Vite insieme*, 15.

Chapter 4

OPEN SOURCE, HACKER SPIRIT, PROPRIETARY INDIVIDUALISM AND ANARCHO-CAPITALISM

The beginnings I: From freedom of speech to freedom of information

If the 1960s were characterized by the birth and spread of hippy culture, the 1980s were characterized by the birth and spread of cyberculture. Cyberculture is the direct offspring of the anti-authoritarian and anti-war movements of the 1960s and early 1970s. It is thus imbued with a libertarian humus that will never wane even when its anti-authoritarian origins are partly abandoned.

We can take as reference two emblematic figures of those years, who will play the role of making cyberculture emerge on an autonomous and even more strictly political level. We speak, in particular, in the field of pioneers, of Stewart Brand and Lee Felsenstein. Both are taken as references as emblems of the hacker spirit that has innervated cyberculture since the early 1970s and are united by having a political vision of the nascent computer science and cybernetics aimed at turning them into instruments of liberation rather than social control to authoritarianism.

Stewart Brand, born thirty years before 1968, after moving to California, made contact with author Ken Kesey (*One Flew Over the Cuckoo's Nest*) and the aforementioned Merry Pranksters, and was one of the organizers (together with Eric Christensen, Ken Kesey himself, Owsley Stanley and Bill Graham[1]) of the first psychedelic rock festival,

---

1. After this experience, Bill Graham, at that time manager of the Mine Troup, a San Francisco theatre company, began to organize shows that attracted elements of the counterculture of the time, such as Jefferson Airplane, Janis Joplin, Country Joe and The Fish, Lawrence Ferlinghetti, The Committee, The

the Trips Festival, which took place from 21 to 23 January 1966 at the Longshoreman's Hall in San Francisco, where the Grateful Dead also performed along with Jefferson Airplane, The Charlatans, The Great Society, The Marbles and Big Brother and the Holding Company with Janis Joplin. It was the first time that live music was also accompanied by psychedelic light shows, mostly created by the Joshua Light Show,[2] about a year before Pink Floyd's famous performances at the UFO Club in London.

Stewart Brand turned his libertarian spirit mainly to the subject of free information and especially the free circulation of images. It may sound naive, but it is not surprising that in 1966 Brand started a public campaign to force NASA to release the controversial images of the Earth seen from space. He believed that everything avant-garde and technologically advanced should be made public to improve the cognitive status of individuals and their ability to interpret the world and be self-determined.

In the wake of this spirit, he came into contact with the circles that were most dedicated to new technologies in the field of data transmission and information. Thus it was that in the late 1960s Brand became an assistant to the electrical engineer Douglas Engelbart, an American computer pioneer and inventor of the first mouse, known for his studies on human-computer interaction and for having developed hypertext, computer networks and the graphic interface with his collaborators.

Based on this experience, Brand became convinced that everyone could have access to free and open information thanks to new models of information transmission that no longer required the intermediation of bureaucratic and power apparatuses that could condition its use or purpose. This gave rise to the idea of the *Whole Earth Catalog*, a container and presentation of everything that could be considered

Fugs, Allen Ginsberg and, most notably, The Grateful Dead. He became the manager of Jefferson Airplane between 1967 and 1968. His successes allowed him to become promoter of major rock concerts. He managed the famous venues of the Fillmore West, Winterland and the Fillmore East (in New York). He died in 1991 at the age of sixty.

2. The Joshua Light Show was a liquid light show that created the well-known psychedelic effects, founded by Joshua White, who had studied electrical engineering, theatrical lighting and magic lantern techniques at Carnegie Tech College at the University of Southern California: http://www.joshualights how.com/.

useful to be able to live better, autonomously and without depending on anyone, in full community and libertarian spirit. It covered books, maps, garden tools, specialized clothing, carpenter's and mason's tools and woodcutter's tools, tents, plumbing tools, specialized newspapers, the first synthesizers and personal computers – the list is long and almost endless. It was a publication that coincided, not surprisingly, with the wave of experimentalism, unconventional and 'do-it-yourself', that was linked to the 'counterculture' of that time and also to the experience of the hippy communes.

The influence of the *Whole Earth Catalog* on the cultural back-to-the-land movement of the 1970s and the community movements of many cities was vast and felt in the United States, Canada and beyond. A 1972 edition sold 1.5 million copies and won the National Book Award in the United States. It was here that many people became acquainted with the possibilities of alternative energy (solar, wind, small-scale hydropower, geothermal) and the issues of ecological-environmental sustainability began to be addressed.

However, the remarkable fact was that the *Catalog* (which came out in four editions until 1986[3]) did not take an anti-technological stance, quite the contrary. It was precisely the technological developments in the field of information technology and cybernetics that opened up new horizons to free man from dependence on machines and the military-industrial apparatus.

The *Catalog* represented the first attempt to make the information necessary for one's life choices usable and accessible through an education programme that was intended to be universal and inexpensive, breaking down those elitist, economic and racial barriers that were at the basis of a profound and emerging cognitive division of labour.[4]

3. The *Last Whole Earth Catalog*, the most successful edition in 1972, was to be the catalogue's last release. But due to the continuous demand for updates and new products it was followed by: *The Whole Earth Epilog* in 1974, *The Updated Last Whole Earth Catalog* in 1975, *The Next Whole Earth Catalog* in 1980 and *The Essential Whole Earth Catalog*, the last publication in 1986. For a more in-depth analysis of this publication, see F. Turner, *From Counterculture to Cyberculture* (Chicago: The University of Chicago Press, 2006), whose subtitle is: *Stewart Brand, The Whole Earth Network and the Rise of Digital Utopianism*.

4. The catalogue has been described as the progenitor of Google by Apple founder Steve Jobs: see https://it.wikipedia.org/wiki/Whole_Earth_Catalog.

The libertarian, solidaristic spirit of the hippy movement was therefore also well represented outside the communities that often experienced processes of self-marginalization.

The beginnings II: Hackers and the computer liberation front

The idea at the basis of Stewart Brand's experiments of free information usable and accessible to all and able to escape any process of control and censorship would find new life a few years later. But its incubation had already begun in the mid-1960s, during the Berkeley uprising and the development of the Free Speech Movement. And it was in that context that a new word was born that was destined to enter the history of philosophy and, in particular, cyberculture: hacker.

Steve Levy, 'author of an accurate historical reconstruction of that pioneering era'[5] in one of his famous books,[6] traces the birth of hackers back to the American Cambridge (Boston) of the 1950s and 1960s and, more precisely, to MIT. And it was precisely in those years, before migrating to California, that the 'hacker spirit' was born and developed: a spirit that energized a community

> which included hardware and software professionals who interpreted their activity as a mission rather than a trade, brilliant amateurs capable of working miracles with the waste products of the electronics industry, politicised technicians and scientists, who came out of the computer industry or government research laboratories to spread their knowledge to the people.[7]

One of these hackers, with a strong political inclination, is certainly Lee Felsenstein, to whom Levy attributes the merit of having been able to unify the two souls of the first hacker movement, the 'aristocratic' one, conscious of holding a particular, almost elitist knowledge, and the 'Jacobin' one, more inclined to contamination and social subversion towards the authoritarian hierarchy dominant at the time.

5. Cf. C. Formenti, *Incantati dalla rete* (Milan: Raffaello Cortina Editore, 2000), 183.

6. Cf. S. Levy, *Hackers. Heroes of the Computer Revolution* (New York: Anchor Press/Doubleday, 1984).

7. Cf. Formenti, *Incantati dalla rete*, 183.

More specifically, Felsenstein breaks with the first hacker generation, all internal to the experimentation of the laboratories of the great university centres on the East Coast. As Levy writes:

Lee Felsenstein felt that he owed nothing to that first generation of hackers. He belonged to a new lineage, he was a hacker of battling, populist hardware. He aimed to bring computers out of the well-protected towers of AI [Artificial Intelligence, Ed.], away from the underground prisons of the accounting departments of large corporations, and thus allow people to discover for themselves the joy of exploring and getting their hands on them.[8]

Felsenstein went on to study engineering at Berkeley in California and afterward had work experience at NASA's Flight Research Center at Edwards Base on the edge of the Mojave Desert, but after two years, he was dismissed because he was suspected – according to McCarthyism's criteria – of being a communist, as his father had been a communist in the past, even though the young student had always declared himself apolitical. It was an important experience, however, that brought him back to Berkeley just as the Free Speech Movement revolt broke out in 1964.

On the night of 14 October 1964, Lee Felsenstein, a failed engineer, took a train back to Berkeley. Lee had heard the news on the radio about the student demonstrations that had been going on there for a fortnight: he took it to be a modern version of the legendary goliardic raids of 1952. But on his return he found the entire community engaged with the Free Speech Movement. 'Secrecy is the keystone of all dictatorships', said the protagonist of Heinlein's Revolt 2100, thus expressing not only the cry of the Berkeley revolution but also the hacker ethos. Lee Felsenstein decided to leap: he went over to the side of the revolutionaries. And he mixed his fervor for the cause with his particular talent. He would use technology to fuel the uprising.[9]

And so it was.

＊ ＊ ＊ ＊ ＊

8. Cf. Levy, *Hackers*, 161.
9. Cf. Levy, *Hackers*, 165.

In the mid-1970s, the first *computer clubs* began to spring up in San Francisco and the surrounding area, places of experimentation and the dissemination of computer culture, often with a twofold purpose: firstly, to familiarize the widest number of people with the new technologies while keeping costs low, and secondly, to break the taboo of technical expertise (the aristocracy of knowledge) and control of information, in the name of freedom of communication and information. On the other hand, the first steps of the computer and digital revolution increasingly sanctioned the centrality of communication and information, and it was precisely in those years that the term ICT (Information, Communication Technology) began to spread.

The battle to make new technologies freely usable was to become the main driving force of the new cyber and open-source movements within a few years.

Thus, a movement developed that did not have its specific name or statute, but consisted of a series of experiments all aimed at the 'liberation of the computer' (computer liberation front). Various are its animators and among them is certainly Lee Felsenstein, who promotes various initiatives to spread computer culture and enable ordinary people to familiarize themselves with computers. The aim is, as he puts it, to combat the industrial approach that favours the monopoly of computer corporations:

> The social approach I suggest should depend on the user's ability to learn to use the tool and master it.[10]

To this end, there are various projects to make technology belong to the people (tech to the people), from taking computers to the streets and allowing people to learn about them for free to create real experiments in multiple connections. Steve Levy recounts one of these experiments, called 'Community Memory', during which several terminals were activated that were freely accessible to the public.

Levy tells it like this:

> People found partners to play chess, to study, to get their snake mated, restaurant and record recommendations were circulated; services such as babysitting, passages, text typing, tarot card reading, plumbing, pantomime and photography were offered …. There were

10. Cf. Levy, *Hackers*, 242.

messages with hermetic quotations from Ginsberg, the Grateful Dead, Arlo Guthrie, Shakespeare.[11]

These were experiments in which it was the cooperation between computer users that triggered processes of sociality, in which the instrument (the computer itself) could prefigure states of openness of the mind:

> the unlimited extension of one's personal imagination, a mirror that emanated no sentences and in which it was possible to frame any kind of desired self-portrait. Regardless of the message, the only imprints the message bore were those of the writer's imagination.[12]

It would be going too far to compare the first uses of the computer to the lysergic trips caused by LSD, even though a statement by Steve Jobs, according to whom his experience with LSD 'was one of the two or three most important things he had ever done in my life', has remained famous. On the other hand, Albert Hofmann himself, the father of LSD, at the age of 101 had written to the Apple CEO in 2009 asking him whether the use of LSD had contributed to his computer creativity, and had received an affirmative reply.[13]

On the other hand, it is sufficiently clear how the computer liberation front was able to activate a kind of social cooperation based on the diffusion of collective knowledge. We thus witness the emergence of one of the first examples of general intellect, as the foundation of a new way of interacting with technology and thus as the basis for a new production model. The digital utopia

11. Cf. Levy, *Hackers*, 181. Note that the Grateful Dead are mentioned.

12. Cf. Levy, *Hackers*, 181.

13. This statement was repeatedly reported on the press. On this, see J. Markoff, *What the Dormouse Said: How the Sixties Counterculture Shaped the Personal Computer Industry* (New York: Penguin Books, 2005). It should be recalled that the FBI, on the orders of Bush senior, issued a 191-page report, made public in 2012, confirming Jobs's drug use. Regarding the correspondence between Hofmann and Jobs, see http://www.huffingtonpost.com/ryan-grim/read-the-never-before-pubb227887. This correspondence is taken from the book by R. Grim, *This Is Your Country on Drugs: The Secret History of Getting High in America* (New Jersey: John Wiley & Sons, 2009). We will return to this aspect in the epilogue to this chapter.

that began to settle in those years sees in the 'democratization of the machinic' and in the possibility of accessing it at a very low cost and in a communitarian manner the principle of a new model of accumulation and production capable of being autonomous and independent of the social and technological hierarchies imposed by the military-industrial apparatus.

It is no longer an exodus seeking new uncontaminated spaces elsewhere from the capitalist system as was the case with the hippy commune, but an attempt to carve out spaces of autonomy and otherness in the capitalist system of production with the intention of detouring it from within. And it is with this transition that we move from counterculture to cyberculture and from Fordist capitalism to an idea of digital capitalism. The 'Jacobin' spirit of the hacker ethos then takes over from the more 'elitist' one.

Learning (free and gratis) and relational networks begin to become the basis of the accumulation and valorization process. These phenomena are by definition social in nature, that is, they imply the development of forms of social cooperation. New ways of organizing work, which will only take hold in the course of the 1980s, characterized by horizontality and teamwork, no longer hierarchized on vertical disciplinary devices, are beginning to be glimpsed. If in Taylorism workplaces were propped up by signs such as 'Quiet, here we work', now it is language, communication, that begins to create value.

> Let us remember the two famous Aristotelian definitions of Homo sapiens: 'animal that has language' and 'political animal'. Animal that has language: verbal speech, an integral part of our biological constitution, qualifies all sorts of affects and perceptions. Political animal: trans-individual (or, if you prefer, public) character of the human mind, its capacity to interact, cooperate, adapt to the possible and the unexpected. Well, it seems to me that the two ancient definitions sum up well what is to be understood by life-at-work. The actual professional skills (so to speak) required of the post-Fordist worker, i.e. the 'flexible man', consist of the faculty of meaning/communication and the faculty of (inter)action.[14]

14. P. Virno, 'Un movimento performativo', April 2005, Available online: http://republicart.net/disc/precariat/virno01_it.htm. See also: P. Virno, *A Grammar of the Multitude. For an Analysis of Contemporary Forms of Life* (Boston, MA: Semiotext(e), MIT Press, 2004).

What at the time was only imaginative power has now become reality. Language implies sociality, at the same time creativity and performativity,[15] but also the need for codification. This codification represents the new form in which fixed capital is reincarnated. Indeed, while physical capital is being downsized, this does not mean that the role of fixed capital is disappearing. In the new digital capitalism, knowledge, insofar as it is separated from every product in which it has been, is or will be incorporated, as when it is mere information and codified practice of communication, can exert a productive action in itself, in the form of standardized language, that is, software: it can, in other words, play the role of fixed capital,[16] thus becoming a sort of 'cognitive machine', substituting stored labour for living labour, whether simple or complex, capable of producing 'cognitive surplus'.[17]

The construction of software, as language, is based on the provision of living labour, which, when it is transformed into an instrument for encoding language ('cognitive machine'), takes on the appearance of dead labour, of fixed capital.

On the other hand, the function of speech, understood as the art of communication, is different. In fact, it allows us to analyse the relationship between individuals not only as an end in itself, but as a productive/performative social process.[18]

Speech is the becoming of language, while language is the codification and systematization of this social production and thus the regulation and normalization of the linguistic creativity of subjects.

15. Cf. J. L. Austin, *How to Do Things with Words: Second Edition (The William James Lectures)* (Cambridge, MA: Harvard University Press, 1975). See also C. Marazzi, *Capital and Language. From the New Economy to the War Economy* (Boston, MA: Semiotext(e), MIT Press, 2008).

16. Cf. C. Marazzi, 'L'ammortamento del corpo-macchina', in *Multitudes* 27 (2007). Available online: https://www.multitudes.net/L-ammortamento-del-corpo-macchina/.

17. The term cognitive surplus would later be used by Clay Shirky (cf. C. Shirky, *Cognitive Surplus: How Technology Makes Consumers into Collaborators* (London: Penguin Putnam Inc., 2011), to indicate 'the surplus of knowledge that is not used in the production process but is continually coveted by companies to ensure technological and organisational innovation', as Bendetto Vecchi writes (cf. B. Vecchi, *La rete dall'utopia al mercato* (Rome: Manifestolibri, 2015), 120.

18. Cf. A. Fumagalli and C. Morini, 'Life Put to Work: Towards a Theory of Life-Value', in *Ephemera* 10, no. 3/4 (2011): 234–52.

We can thus state that the mechanical codification of linguistic practice, as a convention, is today the mechanical element of bioeconomic production, the fixed capital necessary to valorize the living labour of the word as an instrument of communication, relationship, care and affection. This opens up a dialectic between word and language, between living labour and dead labour embedded in the same human body/being.

We define the commons (in the singular) as this dialectical relationship, the outcome of the practice of language and subjective, human relationship, the combination of the 'animal that can speak' and the 'political animal' that defines human nature and whose process of valorization, for it to be at the prerogative of capital, requires a new ownership structure. The commonwealth is thus the basis for the accumulation of digital capitalism.

The commons can take different forms depending on the mode of accumulation, whether it is more based on the exploitation of cognitive-formative faculties or relational-cooperative faculties. To a first approximation, we could call the former the cognitive commonwealth, the latter the re/productive commonwealth.

As we discussed in Chapter 3:[19]

> The commonwealth has nothing to do with the commons: it is simply an expression of the social cooperation that takes place in the general intellect.

The commonwealth was born in California in the second half of the 1970s. And immediately the struggle for its capture and appropriation began.

From digital utopia to anarcho-capitalism

Digital knowledge requires learning and is not immediately given. It is not yet part of the educational system. It means that the methodology of its teaching is still free and has not yet been institutionalized in the rigid syllabus and classroom procedures. In other words, it has not yet fostered a cognitive division of knowledge and thus of labour.

19. Cf. Ch. 3, p. 48.

Moreover, digital knowledge is imbued with active knowledge, not only with *know-how*, the passive learning of an operational technique but also with *know-that*, the understanding and the possession of the processes one is dealing with ('the user's ability to learn how to use the tool and know how to master it', in the words, already quoted, of Lee Felsenstein).[20] The standardization of digital knowledge will come later in the 1990s when the flame of the digital utopia and the dream of subverting the world will be all but extinguished.

Finally, digital knowledge presupposes a new way of understanding the relationship between human being and machines. The digital (virtual) machine enters the human mind and influences it (if only because it imposes a new artificial language), but in the same way, the machinic support to the digital instrument (the computer as a box, pure hardware) is commanded by the human mind through the software that the latter creates and continuously modifies. Only if such a process of command by the human mind (with all its attendant habituation, subalternity, creativity, innovation, subversion) can continually reshape and redefine the artificial language to its use and consumption, then the computer can be an instrument of liberation.

The late 1970s and early 1980s represent the time of the highest level of experimentation in this direction: a direction that intends to keep the door open for the manipulation of languages and forms of communication through the activation of source codes that are never closed and under the control of intellectual property rights.

An example is provided by Ted Nelson, the pioneer of hypertext theories, who, despite not having the technical skills of hackers, was able to design Xanadu over a period of years:

> a huge virtual library connected to a computer network, where anyone could publish whatever they wanted, and 'link' their document with any other in a web of hypertexts.[21].

Nelson was never able to realize his project, which had begun in the early 1960s. But his idea anticipated what would later develop with the World Wide Web. Together with Felsenstein, free access and maximum usability of digital technologies represented the political

20. Quoted by Levy, *Hackers*, 242.

21. Cf. Formenti, *Incantati dalla rete*, 186. Cf. also E. Pedemonte, *Personal Media. Storia e futuro di un'utopia* (Turin: Bollati Boringhieri, 1998), 40ff.

horizon in which computer innovation[22] was to be pursued: free access to information, free access to literature.

Today, Nelson's dream is translated into reality with the Google Books app or other similar forms, but with one difference; intellectual property rights (from patents on source code to copyright on literary works) are well safeguarded and above all monopolistically managed as a source of exchange value.

In contrast, the digital utopia of the 1970s was based on open source at all levels: from basic software to free access to the user interface. And on the fact that there was no predetermined division between tacit and codified knowledge. The former was to be freely put at the service of the community, for all and sundry to enjoy.

Digital freedom was a freedom connected to human freedom of action. Precisely because there is no longer a clear separation between human being and machine since the machine is composed and made operational by the same human living labour (through its cognitive, relational and sentimental faculties), imposing property rights on the human machine meant imposing limitations on human action and social cooperation: the freedom of the general intellect thus became one of the fundamental human freedoms, to be included in the 1948 declaration of human rights.

It is no coincidence that it is precisely this approach that underlies John Perry Barlow's declaration on the independence of cyberspace in the 1990s.[23] And it is with this spirit – the same spirit personified by the psychedelic music of the Grateful Dead – that we approach the decade of the 1980s. And as with the Grateful Dead, this spirit began to be increasingly commodified and above all 'individualized'.

In the group of hackers and activists who revolved around Felsenstein in the various computer clubs, there were also those who a few years later would start the Silicon Valley myth, such as Paul Allen and Bill Gates. And as Steve Levy tells us, regarding the birth of Basic software, of which they were among the main inventors, the two future founders of Microsoft were not very steeped in hacker ethics:

22. In fact, one of Ted Nelson's favourite sayings is: 'A user interface should be so simple that it can be understood, in an emergency, within ten seconds by a novice.'

23. See Chapter 1: cf. John Perry Barlow, 'A Declaration of the Independence of Cyberspace', 1985. Available online: https://vimeo.com/111576518.

[Don] Sokol applied what in hacker terms was the fair rate for software: nothing. The only deal was that you took a tape [with the software, ed.], had to make copies and bring two to the next meeting. He gave them all away. People grabbed the tapes and not only brought copies to the next meeting but also sent them to other computer clubs. So that first version of the Altair Basic was in free circulation even before its official release. There were two hackers, however, who were far from appreciating this demonstration of sharing and cooperation: Paul Allen and Bill Gates. They had sold their Basic to MITS[24] in exchange for a profit per copy sold, and the idea that the hacker community would carelessly reproduce copies of their program and distribute them did not seem particularly utopian to them. Instead, it seemed like theft to them.[25]

This was back in 1975 and 1976 and raised the question of the fairness of royalties (as they were called at the time) on software products. And it is not surprising that Allen and Gates referred to the recording industry, comparing software to a musical product, which could not be openly copied for free, as was the case with the Grateful Dead's live concert tapes.

The debate that ignited within computer clubs – in particular the Homebrew Computer Club[26] (whose members included Apple founders Steve Jobs and Steve Wozniak, who sold copies of their first computer to other members of the club, the Apple I) after the publication of Bill Gates's 'Open Letter to Hobbyists' in January 1976 in favour of royalties

24. Micro Instrumentation and Telemetry Systems, Inc. (abbreviated to MITS) was the American company (from Albuquerque, New Mexico) that produced the first computer, the Altair 8800, in 1975. Basic was the first software language produced for the Altair, hence the name Microsoft.

25. See Levy, *Hackers*, 233–4. The whole story is narrated at https://en.wikipe dia.org/wiki/An_Open_Letter.to-Hobbyists. Sokol, Allen and Gates were the founders of Microsoft.

26. The Homebrew Computer Club was perhaps the best known of the Computer Clubs in the San Francisco Bay Area. Founded in 1975 in Menlo Park, San Mateo County, which acts as a hinge between the southern part of San Francisco and the beginning of the future Silicon Valley, it was a staunch supporter of digital freedom and the possibility of self-made computers. Homebrew, in fact, means 'homemade', in the sense of 'self-made'. Lee Felsenstein also participated assiduously.

for programmers – reintroduced the initial distinction within the hacker movement between the 'aristocratic' and 'Jacobin' sides.

The main question was to what extent the reproduction of a software program, which in any case, still had open codes, could be allowed. On the one hand, it was argued, as Bill Gates did, that the work of the programmer should be remunerated according to the degree of dissemination of the product by means of a kind of copyright (royalties, in fact) as for any artistic or literary work. On the other hand, it was argued that a principle of ownership could not be adopted on an intangible good such as a software program, especially if that product was the result of collective cooperation and exclusively individual effort.

The issue would be resolved when the first computer products, both in terms of software and hardware, were structured on business or individual forms of organization. Computer-digital work thus tends to become an enterprise. And it is in this transition that the question opens up of intellectual property rights, patents, rather than royalties (still a form of remuneration for work performance), and no longer applicable to human activity but to the form of enterprise, thus protecting and safeguarding capital. In this way, technical knowledge is silenced and expropriated within a logic of capitalist commodification.

In any case, the new digital technologies open up prospects for structural change and, even if subsumed within a capitalist logic, can still create spaces of liberation if they are able to escape the forms of control and hierarchies of the military-industrial and state apparatus. Even if the innovation process is increasingly conditioned by a mercantile logic, from the user's point of view, spaces of possible uncontrollable surplus remain open.

The development of virtual networking offered new opportunities in the 1980s and 1990s. From computer communities we move on to virtual communities. If by then the manufacture of hardware and the production of software had become increasingly a monopoly of the nascent corporations of Silicon Valley or Boston's Route 126, the same could not be said for the colonization of virtual space.

The non-existence of borders in the World Wide Web made any attempt at enclosure, at least in the short term, impossible.

The year of the turning point was 1985 (just as 1975, ten years earlier, had been the year of the birth of the first computer clubs). It is in fact in that year that the first virtual community, the WELL (Whole Earth 'Lectronic Link), a network of interconnected computers, founded by Stewart Brand (him again) and the computer entrepreneur Larry Brilliant, was launched. Brand's new creature, an offspring of the Whole

Earth Catalog experience, aimed to create a web-based community discussion space to promote products, activities and actions that would help individuals find their guide to creating their own living environment by sharing the experience with anyone interested.

The WELL's charter was still very much tied to the counterculture themes of the 1960s. Most of its members were Deadheads and the main community leaders, besides Brand himself, such as Matthew McClure, John Coate (for a time marketing director) and Cliff Figallo, came from experiences of the hippy communes of the 1970s – in particular, the commune Farm, founded by an English professor at San Francisco State University, Stephen Gaskin, in Summertown, Tennessee.[27] Also in the same year, the Media Lab of the MIT (Massachusetts Institute of Technology) in Cambridge (Boston) was founded and developed, under the propulsive drive of Nicholas Negroponte.

These are two very different experiences, however. In the WELL community, the prevailing spirit is still libertarian, while in the MIT Media Lab, the aim is to promote innovation for business purposes: the liberalist spirit dominates to the detriment of the libertarian one.

A synthesis of these two experiences is provided by Kevin Kelly, the leading intellectual of *Wired*, founded among others by Negroponte, the magazine that best synthesizes the libertarian-capitalist (libertarian) positions of the new digital era.

In his book *Out of Control*,[28] Kelly argues that digital technology (ICT), unlike Taylorist technology, is not meant to control social evolution, but rather to create the horizontal and flexible platform that could be the basis on which society itself could evolve. The horizontality of the network, as opposed to the verticality of static and mechanical technologies, is the outcome of a structure built from billions of mechanical, cultural, biological elements that functions and evolves as a kind of living super-organism. And it is as if the new technology

27. Cf. E. Turner, *From Counterculture to Cyberculture: Stewart Brand, the Whole Earth Network, and the Rise of Digital Utopianism* (Chicago: University of Chicago Press, 2008), 147. Turner writes: 'even for the former citizens of the Farm, the WELL became a system to be managed according to a mix of cybernetic principles. On the WELL, human and technical systems existed simultaneously in interaction with one another and, at a theoretical level at least, as mirrors of one another' (147).

28. Cf. K. Kelly, *Out of Control: The New Biology of Machines* (London: Fourth Estate (HarperCollins), 1995).

moulds social evolution in its own image, with a far greater degree of democracy.

However, Kelly reiterates that this machinic and reticular order (the human becoming of the network) evolves randomly and chaotically, without any rules. Especially with regard to economic dynamics, we are in the presence of a constant process of selection, adaptation and modification of routines reminiscent of the Darwinian evolution of the species. The link with the evolutionary theories of business is obvious.[29]

Digital technology (and with it, society) evolves on the basis of a dialectical process between individual human action (the entrepreneurial spirit of the various Gates, Jobs, etc.) and the reaction of the environment, increasingly represented by the market order, which, as Kelly acknowledges, has now completely supplanted the community spirit of the original hacker populism. Rather than the invisible hand of Adam Smith, despite a famous quotation from Bill Gates, we are faced on the one hand with the Schumpeter of 'creative destruction' and on the other with an idea of the market as an organization à la von Hayek.[30]

29. Cf. R. Nelson and S. Winter, *An Evolutionary Theory of Technical Change* (Boston: Belknap Press, 1982).

30. Carlo Formenti, in his *Incantati dalla rete*, insists on analysing the capitalist-liberal drift of the IT world by referring to Adam Smith's free market theory (192). To back this up, Formenti cites Bill Gates's speech announcing the birth of Friction Free Capitalism, paying homage to Adam Smith himself: 'In 1776, describing the concept of the market, Adam Smith theorized that if every buyer knew the price demanded by every seller and if every seller knew how much every buyer was willing to pay, everyone operating in the market would be able to make decisions on the basis of complete information and social resources would be distributed efficiently' (quoted in E. Pedemente, *Personal Media. History and Future of a Utopia* (Turin: Bollati Boringhieri, 1998), 183, speech delivered in Seattle in 1997). In reality, every (serious) economist knows perfectly well that the hypothesis of perfect and complete information does not exist and that, as the other great free market theorist Friedrich von Hayek argued, economic exchange always takes place under conditions of uncertainty (an uncertainty that cannot be eliminated even by access to the web) and that it is precisely prices, if left free to fluctuate, that provide the missing information for economic exchange to be as efficient as possible. Thus, the market is not the place where individuals with equal opportunities and knowledge meet, but rather the place where market hierarchies are continually being redefined, hierarchies that, according to von Hayek, reward the most enterprising.

In this way, the anarcho-capitalist vision develops, caught between many ambiguities and contradictions, which however leads to the end of the anti-authoritarian liberation dream of the first 'computer for the people' or 'computer liberation front' movements.

Instead, the subject of network democracy and digital freedoms and rights remains open.

Today, the process of industrialization of immaterial computer production is becoming more and more established, whereby industrialization is meant, according to Romano Alquati's definition:

> the collective and scientifically organised way of acting/working, which is based on the machinery as a material basis and on innovation and the progressive saving of work/activity and time.[31]

In the computer industry, the machinery – as already emphasized – tends to take on an anthropogenic dimension, a mix of body and mind, of material and immaterial. However, this does not detract from the fact that, today, it favours the growth of increasingly serial and repetitive work processes and less and less creative work processes, at least in relation to the 1980s of its birth and first diffusion.[32]

Less well established, however, is the issue of network access and freedom of use. The cognitive division of labour that the industrialization of ICT sectors favours on the production side does not automatically translate to the demand side.

If one does not consider the digital divide, theoretically every individual in possession of a computer and a connection can access virtual space more or less equally.

Differences manifest themselves in the costs and barriers that may limit their use, citing reasons of protection, secrecy and privacy or even ethical factors (as in the case of child pornography sites).

As is well known, the debate on the regulation of the internet, on the extension and/or limitation of intellectual property rights, and on

---

31. R. Alquati, *Lavoro e attività* (Rome: Manifestolibri, 1997). For a more in-depth discussion on the topic of the 'industrialization' of cognitive labour and ICT production, see S. Cominu, 'Cognitive Labour and Industrialization', *Sudcomune*, no. 0 (2015): 30–41.

32. Cf. S. Baldwin and B. Lessard, *Netslaves* (New York: McGraw Hill, 1999); C. Formenti, *Felici e sfruttati. Capitalismo digitale ed eclissi del lavoro* (Milan: Egea, 2011); Vecchi, *La rete dall'utopia al mercato*.

the monopolies that may derive from it, is very wide-ranging, and this is not the place to repeat it. Here we limit ourselves to recalling that on this front the libertarian battle in the United States has been particularly lively since the writings of Bruce Sterling[33] up to the foundation of the Electronic Free Foundation by Barlow. This battle is still going on today and finds its roots directly in the anti-authoritarian counterculture of the 1960s.

* * * * *

There is no doubt that the revolution of new technologies, born out of the drive for greater independence, autonomy and freedom from the hierarchical and power devices inherent in US military and economic governance, has produced a hybrid between an effective process of liberation thanks to the new opportunities granted, and at the same time a return to the individualism of the frontier, of self-reliance, typical of the American spirit since the Far West of the nineteenth century. This undoubtedly constitutes a not inconsiderable spur to change and innovation, but always within a capitalist relationship of production, dictated by the prevalence of proprietary individualism. Individual freedom and private property, closely intertwined, define the spirit of capitalism.

The novelty that the information technology revolution forcefully posed, and which at its dawning had hinted at the possibility that the tension towards social transformation and change in human relations could decline outside the individualized and privatized relations inherent to capitalism, lay in the cooperative and relational nature of a technology that did not contemplate hierarchical and vertical models, but which based its very capacity for transformation on the free and conscious horizontality of social cooperation.

Pierre Lévy, in his well-known book,[34] highlights the contradiction between the pollution of neo-liberal ideology and the development of the computer industry, driven by the use of the ideal principles of the hacker movement. It is precisely this dialectic that is at the same time the engine of technological progress:

---

33. Cf. B. Sterling, *The Hacker Crackdown: Law and Disorder on the Electronic Frontier* (New York: Bantam Books, 1992).

34. Cf. P. Lévy, *Cyberculture* (Minneapolis: University of Minnesota Press, 2001).

The intertwining of cyber-business with other production and exchange activities is now such that the existence and development of the Internet (with the typical characteristics of its communication device) are now almost completely guaranteed. Business has consolidated and made irreversible what utopia had begun to build. Let us add that many cyber entrepreneurs of the cyber economy are also network visionaries .... The growth of cyberculture is fuelled by a dialectic of utopia and business, in which each tries to play the other without, for the moment, any losers.[35]

Along the same lines of reasoning, in search of a perhaps impossible compromise, Kelly[36] also puts himself forward when he states that the hacker spirit has nevertheless remained in action even within what Lévy called cyber-business.

The aspect that Kelly captures is the element of passion and gratuitousness. That same element of passion and sharing has animated Deadheads for decades in their search for a world of perceptions and possibilities that has always animated the actions of multitudinous movements from 1968 onwards, especially present in the 1977 movement in Italy: the perception that one lives today and 'of tomorrow there is no certainty'. It is the same passion (illusorily aimed at the production of use-value) that was at the basis of the greatest innovations in thought and technology and that today, twenty years later, remains more or less unchanged in the idea of the construction of the 'common' and, paradoxically, of the 'new man', already preconceived by Lenin in the days of Nep in the aftermath of the Bolshevik Revolution of 1917.

This passion – as history has amply demonstrated to us, even in recent decades – has overflowed into 'stupid' gratuitousness, while the quest for positive flexibility has turned into precariousness, and the liberation and rejection of and from work into new, even more, sophisticated forms of exploitation and alienation.

In the more strictly economic context, a new contradiction arises: the new learning- and network-based technologies use inputs that are not by nature scarce, or at least are as 'scarce' as human beings are. Knowledge, in fact, is not a rival good: the more it is exchanged and spread, the more abundant it becomes. A theory of value based on the

35. Lévy, *Cyberculture*, 199.

36. Cf. K. Kelly, *New Rules for the New Economy: 10 Ways the Network Economy is Changing Everything* (London: Fourth Estate Ltd (HarperCollins), 1999).

concept of scarcity, such as that based on the market law of supply and demand, now loses any reason to exist within the hypothesis of bio-cognitive capitalism.

In fact, Kelly (and not only he[37]) wonders:

> To this day, digital impulses, stock subscription rights, copyrights and trademarks have no measurable form (value, ed.). What is the unit of measurement of software: the floppy disk? The strings of code? The number of programs? The number of configurations?[38]

Kelly wrote this in 1999. Today, we might ask ourselves: how much is a 'like' on Facebook or a 'follow' on Twitter worth? How much is a Google query worth? How much is a shopping bill at a supermarket checkout with a loyalty card or watching a TV programme worth?

It is clear that today, in the universe of ICT, the internet, social media, our whole life is put to value. A life that is not scarce, far from it. Because if capitalism is able to feed on the valorization of a single individual's life, which sooner or later is destined to die, it is the whole of human collectivity that continues to reproduce itself in an enlarged manner to the point of becoming the basis of accumulation and individual and corporate proprietary valorization.

The individual is a source of value, not only as an individual; rather, only when acting collectively, but denying that collective cooperation. Hence the capitalist expropriation of the hacker ethic, of social cooperation, of the commons: ultimately, the Grateful Dead economics.

Hence the great fraud of the internet as a space of liberation. And the premises are developed for the solidification of libertarian and anarcho-capitalist thought, highlighting two opposing strands.

Both start from an anti-authoritarian approach and a critique of the role of control over the individual owner played by the state or any public institution. But if the anarcho-capitalist approach also fights against the new role assumed by the great private capitalism of corporations, in favour of digital freedom and for a free, but not necessarily unpaid, access to technology with a strong limitation of intellectual property rights (open source), the more classic liberalist approach moves towards the primacy of the market, regardless of the more or less hegemonic role that the main actors may assume, within rules defined by an anti-trust.

37. Cf. Fumagalli and Morini, 'Life Put to Work'.
38. Cf. Kelly, *New Rules for the New Economy*, 9.

On the one hand, it is personal freedom and freedom of action that counts, on the other hand, it is market competition that is the element to be preserved. Libertarianism and liberalism are not synonymous.

But, in any case, such a debate never questions the foundations of the capitalist system of production: private property in the form of proprietary individualism and the capital-labour relationship as a source of valorization and accumulation, that is, the exploitation of man on man.

At the limit, the anarcho-capitalist, libertarian approach is more in favour of the fact that within a capitalist system there can also be, in a complementary manner, spaces and areas for the production of use-value, thus not exclusively destined for the production of profit, something that instead appears completely absent in the libertarian approach, where it is individual profit (thus the sole production of exchange-value) that is the driving force of accumulation.

The galaxy of anarcho-capitalism and the cyberpunk movement: the foundations of Grateful Dead economics

Libertarian positions are varied and manifold. One can find a little bit of everything. From the position that advocates the abolition of the monopoly of money issuance thanks to the new technological opportunities offered by electronic money (cryptocurrency),[39] to those of a neo-Luddite stamp, who see in information technology and the figure of the cyborg the risk of the machinic overpowering human nature to the point of enslaving it (Matrix model), to the cyber-punk position.

We will not dwell on the former, but on the cyberpunk counterculture, which also in Italy played an important role within the antagonist movements from the 1980s onwards. The cyberpunk strand is the one that mostly picked up the political legacy of the hacker movement, following a direction opposed to the naturalism and technophobia of the previous generation (and the neo-Luddites).

In the movement's manifesto – the anthology *Mirrorshades* published in 1986 – Bruce Sterling claims a kind of new alliance

---

39. This topic will be the subject of the next chapter.

between technologies and countercultures,[40] highlighting the kind of 'out-of-control' excess evoked by Kelly.

In the preface to the anthology, Sterling writes:

The traditional power structure, the traditional institutions, have lost control of the pace of change. And suddenly a new alliance is becoming evident: an integration of technology and the Eighties counterculture. An unholy alliance of the technical world and the world of organized dissent-the underground world of pop culture, visionary fluidity, and street-level anarchy.[41]

And a little further on:

The counterculture of the 1960s was rural, romanticized, anti-science, anti-tech. But there was always a lurking contradiction at its heart, symbolized by the electric guitar. Rock technology was the thin edge of the wedge. As the years have passed, rock tech has grown ever more accomplished, expanding into high-tech recording, satellite video, and computer graphics. ... As Alvin Toffler pointed out in *The Third Wave* – a bible to many cyber punks – the technical revolution reshaping our society is based not in hierarchy but in decentralization, not in rigidity but in fluidity.[42]

The hacker and the rocker are this decade's pop-culture idols, and cyberpunk is very much a pop phenomenon: spontaneous, energetic, close to its roots. Cyberpunk comes from the realm where the computer hacker and the rocker overlap, a cultural Petri dish where writhing gene lines splice.[43]

The analogy between the hacker and the rocker is interesting. Music thus becomes the bridge between an anarchic vision of digital technology and the organization of a dissent that is confronted with the emergence of new forms of power based on intellectual property rights and new forms of hierarchization of life and commodification of existing life.

40. Cf. B. Sterling, *Mirrorshades: The Cyberpunk Anthology* (Ipswich: Arbor House, 1986)

41. Sterling, *Mirrorshades*, xii (preface).

42. Sterling, *Mirrorshades*, xii.

43. Sterling, *Mirrorshades*, xiii.

Unlike the counterculture of the 1960s, the cyberpunk movement has a minor political connotation, especially in the United States.[44] In the 1990s it grew into a detachment from the forms of traditional official politics to such an extent that many exponents of cyberpunk and the practice of social hacking make no secret, in the name of the anarchic-individualist culture, of preferring to vote for Republican Party candidates rather than Democratic Party candidates, who are more ready to justify the economic interventionism of the state. The Republican Party, especially in some radical fringes, is seen as a better defender of personal freedoms against the invasive presence of state bureaucracy and forms of economic regulation of a collective-welfare nature.

A resounding example is provided by John Perry Barlow, founder and president of the Free Electronic Frontier, as well as lyricist of the Grateful Dead themselves. In 1978, he served as chairman of the Republican Party for Sublette County and was campaign coordinator for Dick Cheney in western Wyoming in the same year. In the early 2000s, Barlow 'was unable to reconcile his ardent libertarianism with the prevailing neoconservative movement, and "didn't feel tempted to vote for Bush"'.[45]

If the Barlow case is emblematic of a certain attitude in the relationship between the libertarian movement of an anarchic nature and liberal thought (best represented by the Democrats), it should also be noted that in the cyberpunk movement one can recognize, albeit partially, the origins of the black bloc movement that began to spread in the United States in the mid-1990s.[46]

44. In Europe and, above all, in Italy, thanks to the work of the magazine *Decoder,* the cyberpunk movement is closely connected with the area of the self-managed social centres that proliferated throughout the country in the aftermath of the so-called 'panther' movement of the late 1980s (which marked the end of the Italian middle ages after the defeat of the social and protest movements of the 1970s). For a detailed history, up to the early 2000s, see A. Di Corinto and T. Tozzi, *Hacktivism. La libertà nelle maglie della rete* (Rome: Manifestolibri, 2002), esp. para. 3.4.2, Social Hacking and Cyberpunk. Available online: http://www.hackerart.org/storia/hacktivism/3_4_2.htm.

45. https://en.wikipedia.org/wiki/John_Perry_Barlow.

46. The Black Bloc is a protest tactic, not a formal organization, involving masked, black-clad protesters who use anonymity to protect identities and potentially engage in property destruction or clashes with police, often linked to anarchist and anti-fascist movements seeking to disrupt capitalism and state power. See: https://en.wikipedia.org/wiki/Black_bloc

Towards new models of labour organization and wage regulation

The spread of digital culture (Netculture[47]) and ICT technologies has profoundly changed the organization of work. The horizontal nature of the new IT paradigm breaks away from the vertical-hierarchical plan that has always characterized Taylorist work organization based on the rigidly predefined sequence: design → execution → realization.

As pointed out earlier, one of the essential features of today's bio-cognitive capitalism is the dematerialization of fixed capital and the transfer of its productive and organizational functions into the living body of labour-power.

This process is at the origin of one of the paradoxes of the new capitalism, namely the contradiction between the increasing importance of cognitive labour as a lever of wealth production and, at the same time, its devaluation in terms of both wages and jobs. This paradox is internal to what Marazzi in one of his essays called 'the anthropogenic character of contemporary capitalist production'.[48] In bio-cognitive capitalism, the living being contains within itself both the functions of fixed capital and variable capital, that is, of material and tools of past labour and present living labour: the bios. It follows that the separation between abstract and concrete labour is no longer as clear-cut as in industrial-Fordist capitalism.

First of all, today what Marx called concrete labour, the labour that produces use-values, can be renamed creative labour. In fact, this term allows us to better grasp the cerebral contribution inherent in such activity, while the term 'concrete labour', although conceptually synonymous, refers more to the idea of 'doing' than 'thinking', with a more marked reference to craft work in and of itself.

47. Cf. T. Terranova, *Network Culture* (Rome: Manifestolibri, 2006).

48. Cf. C. Marazzi, 'Digital Capitalism and the Anthropogenic Model of Work. The Depreciation of the Machine Body', in J. L. Laville, C. Marazzi, M. La Rosa and F. Chicchi (eds), *Reinventing Work* (Rome: Sapere 2000, 2005), 107–26. Here is the full quote regarding the concept of the anthropogenetic model of production: 'a model, that is, of the production of human through human, in which the possibility of endogenous and cumulative growth is given above all by the development of the educational sector (investment in human capital), the health sector (demographic evolution, biotechnologies) and the cultural sector (innovation, communication and creativity)' (109).

The so-called creative work does not immediately refer to the concept of the creative class.[49] On the contrary, it is precisely the new condition of cognitive work that is based on the heterogeneity of the subjects put to work, especially when it is subjectivity (singularity) itself that is put to value. This does not allow for the formation of a homogeneous class, in and of itself, but rather a multitude of differentiated singularities, each with its own working perception.

One of the effects of the new computer technology paradigm, precisely because it changes the relationship between mankind and machine, is that it does not allow for the formation of social classes that the twentieth century handed down to us. At the limit, we can speak of the working condition (in particular the precarious condition).

It is also this production of new subjectivities that heavily affects mechanisms of self-control, governance and self-repression, on the one hand, and illusion, meritocracy and indebtedness, on the other.

In bio-cognitive capitalism, moreover, we are increasingly witnessing an interpenetration between place of production and production networks.

Space, geographical and virtual, becomes the locus of production no longer characterized by a single, self-centred presence, but rather by sets of polycentric formal and informal networks. Production is the outcome of a flow structure, increasingly immaterial or within which immaterial networks are those that design and direct it, even and especially when the commodity produced is material. A flow structure presupposes the centrality of linguistic communication networks and the development of social cooperation. This cooperation concerns both the transmission of symbols and the logistical transport of goods and commodities. Within this space, however, cooperation, far from being horizontal, develops along new trajectories of spatial division of production and cognitive division of labour. That is, the networked production is a molecular, individualized space, characterized by individual relationships that most often produce downstream cooperation but are not necessarily cooperative with each other.

As a result of these transformations, the production of value is no longer based on a homogeneous and standardized scheme of labour organization, regardless of the type of good produced.

49. Cf. R. Florida, *The Rise of the Creative Class: And How It's Transforming Work, Leisure, Community and Everyday Life* (New York: Basic Books, 2002).

Production activity takes place in different organizational modes, characterized by a network structure, thanks to the development of linguistic communication and transport technologies. The result is a disruption of the traditional unilateral hierarchical form within the factory, which is replaced by hierarchical structures that are implemented in the territory along subcontracting production chains, characterized by cooperation and/or command relationships.

It follows that, in bio-cognitive capitalism, the division of labour also takes on cognitive characteristics; that is, it is based on the differentiated use and access of different forms of knowledge.

Knowledge can be divided into four levels: information, codified knowledge, tacit knowledge and culture (or systemic knowledge), characterized by unilateral dependency relationships.[50]

Information is the basic level of knowledge that is increasingly embedded in the machine element. Codified knowledge is that specialized knowledge (know-how) that derives from tacit knowledge but is transmitted through standardized procedures, with the intermediation of machines, and the consequence that the bearer of this knowledge can be replaced at any time, without being able to leverage some form of bargaining power. Tacit knowledge can arise from personal learning processes or from specific investments in R&D (thanks to intellectual property rights); moreover, at least until it becomes codified, it cannot be transmitted other than through human beings, with the possibility of originating forms of enclosures. Those who possess tacit knowledge, relevant to the production process, thus hold a high bargaining power and define the hierarchical structure in production and work. However, tacit knowledge, if relevant, is destined sooner or later to turn into codified knowledge and thus to be devalued. Culture, finally, is the totality of those knowledges and skills that enable the intellectual function, that is, critical and creative activity, not immediately subsumed under the logic of bio-capitalist valorization. Consequently, it is dangerous for the socio-economic survival of the system, but it also the main source of value creation, provided that it is controlled.

Finally, the condition of the labour force is accompanied by mobility and the predominance of individual bargaining (precariousness). This stems from the fact that it is the nomadic individualities that are

---

50. Cf. A. Fumagalli, *Bioeconomia e capitalismo cognitivo* (Rome: Carocci, 2007).

put to work, and the primacy of private law over labour law leads to transforming the contribution of individualities, especially those characterized by cognitive, relational and affective activities, into contractual individualism. The employment relationship based on the condition of precariousness, that is, temporal limitation and spatial mobility of work performance, is the basic paradigm of today's form of the capital-labour relationship. Precariousness thus becomes a structural, existential and generalized condition.

In such a framework, necessarily only sketched out, more flexible models of work organization develop, capable of rapid adaptability to changes in the economic and social context.

We are not referring – as one might think according to the prevailing common sense – to labour flexibility alone, but in particular to the flexibility of command at work, an aspect that is rarely emphasized, especially in Europe and Italy.

In the United States, individual bargaining (with its side effects on job precarity/flexibility) has always played a dominant role over collective bargaining. This is particularly true in the newly emerging ICT sectors, where qualitative changes in work performance induce greater individual participation and involvement in the production process.

As we have already pointed out, the boundary between labour and capital (but also between concrete and abstract labour) is no longer as clearly traceable as before.

The way in which labour is remunerated also tends to change. The new IT companies formally take on the connotation of stakeholder companies, that is, companies for which maintaining a virtuous and positive relationship with suppliers, employees and customers is of fundamental strategic importance. In fact they tend to be more shareholder companies, that is, companies whose primary objective is to increase shareholder value and listed share capital.

This is the outcome of the process of financialization that marked the advent of the new bio-cognitive capitalism and that favoured what Carlo Vercellone called: 'the becoming rent of profit',[51] the result of the process of expropriation of productive cooperation induced by the

51. Cf. C. Vercellone, 'The Crisis of the Law of Value and the Becoming Rent of Profit', in A. Fumagalli and S. Mezzadra (eds), *Crisis in the Global Economy. Financial Markets, Social Struggle and New Political Scenarios* (Cambridge, MA: MIT Press, 2010), 85–118.

exploitation of network and learning economies, the two new dynamic economies of scale that underpin productivity gains, especially in the presence of immaterial production.

It is, in fact, through the new role of the financial markets (or, rather, of the oligarchies that dominate them), capable of defining and directing today's dominant financial conventions,[52] that dot.com companies since the early 1990s have been self-financing themselves with the capital gains generated by payback operations, leverage buy-outs,[53] mergers and acquisitions, and so on, on their shares.

In this way, the financial markets become the engine of accumulation and valorization of the IT industry and the internet, both in terms of how continuous innovation is financed and how income is distributed. More and more employees are seeing productivity gains remunerated with shareholdings. Thus, we are also witnessing the becoming rent of wages.

It is these new modes of financing that, together with a more cooperative organization of work (without, however, the hierarchy breaking down), where the workforce is involved to a greater extent in the design and production process, allow the boom of the so-called net economy in the 1990s in the United States and the rise in the following decade of the great industrial giants linked to social, media and internet surfing, and the collection and processing of increasingly imposing databases (big data).

In this organization of production, a central role is played by the consumer, whose individuality increasingly becomes a direct source of value.

52. It was Keynes (cf. J. M. Keynes, *General Theory of Employment, Interest and Money* (London: Macmillan, 1936), especially ch. XII) who introduced the term *financial convention* to describe an upward or downward trend that could steer the stock markets thanks to convergent expectations (positive or negative) driven by the interests of the main and most influential speculators.

53. These are financial techniques that aim at the expected increase in the shares of a listed company so that positive capital gains can be made. The term payback refers to the sale or purchase of one's own shares (by the company's manager) in order to boost the company's share price. Leverage buy-out means acquisition through debt, through a complex series of transactions between the management of the two companies involved. The site is usually an increase in the share value of the acquiring company: https://en.wikipedia.org/wiki/Lev eraged_ buyout.

It is no coincidence that the term prosumer (consumer-producer) was first coined in 1980 by Toffler in his book *The Third Wave*, remembered by Sterling as a kind of bible for the cyberpunk movement.

It should be noted, however, that in cyberpunk literature, the idea of the prosumer indicated the consumer-producer rather than the producer-consumer, within that libertarian utopia that advocated a democratization of production to such an extent that the generation of use-value should take precedence over the generation of exchange-value.

Recent history tells us that things have not turned out exactly this way.

Epilogue

We quote as a conclusion to this chapter an article by John Clarke published on 30 April 2012 in the well-known magazine for managers, *Forbes*.[54] Just under thirteen years after the death of Steve Jobs and nineteen after that of Jerry Garcia, the article asks whether Jerry Garcia can be considered the Steve Jobs of rock and roll. A parallel that perhaps explains better than any essay the parable of the anti-authoritarian movement from the 1960s to the present.

Jerry Garcia of the Grateful Dead: 'The Steve Jobs of rock and roll'?

by John Clarke.

A former Grateful Dead manager says the late Jerry Garcia is a lot like Steve Jobs in terms of business leadership skills.

'The Grateful Dead's business model is increasingly becoming something of a guide for contemporary industry', writes Sam Cutler,[55]

54. Cf. http://www.forbes.com/sites/johnclarke/2012/04/30/grateful-deads-jerry-garcia-the-steve-jobs-of-rock-and-roll/.

55. Sam Cutler was one of the 'masters of ceremonies' of very famous concerts (Eric Clapton with Cream, Pink Floyd), including the Rolling Stone's free concert in Hyde Park, London, in July 1969, as well as the entire world tour. After the tragedy at the Altamont Festival in October 1969, where the Hell's Angel security guard (expressly wanted by the British rock band) stabbed an African-American boy to death for trivial reasons, Sam Cutler linked up with Jerry Garcia and became the Grateful Dead's road manager from the early 1970s.

examining what made the Grateful Dead's experiences relevant to today's companies. 'Whatever the model of the Grateful Dead was, it would have been inconceivable without Jerry Garcia.'

Garcia, the band's legendary guitarist who died of a heart attack in 1995, practised a form of 'benevolent despotism' in which the band and employees recognised that 'he was irreplaceable and a worthy recipient of collective trust', Cutler writes.

'I can think of no CEO who can compare to Garcia in the contemporary business landscape. Only Warren Buffet and Steve Jobs are the only two, in my opinion, who can match him, and neither of them ever played in a band. Like Garcia they simply ran their businesses with unparalleled personal power and authority.

The approach of Buffet and Jobs was based on a strong charismatic image as it was for Jerry: Berkshire Hathaway and Apple (and Grateful Dead) seem to have worked on the principle that anything was right as long as the "boss" agreed. This allowed flexibility and innovation in an environment where people's ideas were valued and considered as effective assets rather than nuisances.

They were undoubtedly well predisposed towards organised chaos, so they were naturally flexible. That flexibility has been one of the reasons for the band's success and', adds Cutler, 'it is a quality that is sorely lacking in today's business world. The Dead had the "ability to keep their feet on the ground, to change their approach when it became unsatisfactory, to change their strategic planning in a short period of time, and to pursue a commitment to the community including employees, rather than the pure pursuit of naked self-interest".

Another key aspect of the Dead's business model was the involvement of customers, or, in this case, Deadheads.

The priority for the Dead was to make sure that their fans (their customer base, if you like) always felt involved and satisfied with the band's activities. The Dead made music with them and for them and every Deadhead felt intimately connected to the band's activities.'

Finally, Cutler could not resist pointing out another obvious similarity between Garcia and Jobs: LSD consumption. Garcia's intake is well documented and Jobs called his experience with LSD 'one of the two or three most important things I've done in my life'.

Cutler writes: 'The only CEO of a major company, to my knowledge, who willingly credited some of his successes and ideas to LSD was Steve Jobs', he writes. 'You can think what you like about it. It would be brave to suggest to the captains of American industry to take acid! But can this be said in the current economic climate?

Many of the old business models are obsolete and need a thorough rethinking. They need to be fearlessly re-examined and those parts of the model that no longer work need to be discarded or at least substantially modified. In short – throw out the old and bring in the new – and in the unlikely event that it is not broken, don't even fix it!'

Chapter 5

THE MONEY OF THE COMMONWEALTH AND THE FINANCIAL COUNTERCULTURE

The failure of the barter economy in the hippy counterculture

The maximum development of counterculture movements and protests against social and State authoritarianism in the United States, Europe and other regions of the world took place in the early 1970s, even if in West Coast California (where it all began) the transition to the new decade marked the beginning of the decline, not so much in terms of quantitative participation but in terms of qualitative alternative propositions.

Once again, the Grateful Dead are the interpreters of this transition with their turn from pure psychedelic rock to country music, in search of a more intimate habitat and a more communitarian and collected *modus vivendi*: almost a return to the more traditional roots of the (white) American people.

And it was in this communal setting, represented by the hippy commune, that the first alternative forms of payment began to be experimented with. At the end of the 1960s, when the commune represented an elsewhere, capable of being completely autonomous from the capitalist commodification of the military-industrial apparatus, the rejection of money as a means of payment was the natural consequence. In a closed circuit, with no economic relations outside the confines of the commune, exchange was eminently barter based on a theory of value that could only refer to the labour theory of value, on the model of today's 'time banks'.

Money, however, shows us that the human being is a social animal. Money is social relations. A social relation that is mediated and commanded by the capitalist structure of production is, however, an unequal social relation. Money is, above all, power. Power of decision, power of will.

And in the 1960s, at the height of the development of the Taylorist-Fordist paradigm, the availability of access to money (in its monetary form) defines the class structure of society and the division not only of labour but also of symbols.

The aversion to the use of money depends not only on socio-political motivations (money as an instrument of power and economic discrimination) but also and above all on its role as an instrument of the commodification of human beings and their creative potential: it becomes an instrument of biopolitical control and the production of imaginary.

The well-known words of the young Marx from the *Economic & Philosophic Manuscripts of 1844* come to mind:

> That which is for me through the medium of *money* – that for which I can pay (i.e., which money can buy) – that am *I myself*, the possessor of the money. The extent of the power of money is the extent of my power. Money's properties are my – the possessor's – properties and essential powers. Thus, what I *am* and *am capable of* is by no means determined by my individuality. I *am* ugly, but I can buy for myself the *most beautiful* of women. Therefore, I am not *ugly*, for the effect of *ugliness* – its deterrent power – is nullified by money. I, according to my individual characteristics, am *lame*, but money furnishes me with twenty-four feet. Therefore, I am not lame. I am bad, dishonest, unscrupulous, stupid; but money is honoured, and hence its possessor. Money is the supreme good, therefore its possessor is good.[1]

In the capitalist system of production, moreover, money becomes an expression of capital and of the social relationship of labour exploitation. In Taylorist-Fordist capitalism, the main function of money is credit within a M-C-M system (money-commodities-money, that is, monetary economy of production), where investment activity in the production of goods requires monetary anticipation and indebtedness of economic actors (be they private enterprises or the state) based on

---

1. Cf. K. Marx, *Economic & Philosophic Manuscripts of 1844*, third manuscript, ch. 'The Power of Money', fr. XLII. Available online: https://www.marxists.org/archive/marx/works/1844/manuscripts/power.htm

the founding principle of the capitalist system itself, according to which without indebtedness there is no accumulation.

Access to credit-money is therefore a factor of social power, which only enterprises and the State can enjoy due to their ownership status. Businesses can offer the guarantee of ownership of the means of production (and subsequently intellectual property), the State has the monopoly of issuing money (seigniorage rights) through the Central Bank, the only institution that can print money without any absolute constraint other than the – relative – constraint of economic compatibility.

The refusal to use money as a means of payment thus has a twofold objective: to reject the economic hierarchy imposed by the social relationship between capital and labour that access to money imposes and, at the same time, to reject the hegemonic role of the State form as the regulatory body which, through its monopoly of the power of issuance, defines the unity of value of the credit function of money and thus its being a means of payment and a unit of account.

However, a return to pure bartering is impossible, unless it locks us into areas of marginality and separation from the rest of the world. Certainly – as we have already argued, in Chapter 3 – such a return is one of the possible preconditions for exodus, aimed at experimenting with new alternative models of life, but it is not sufficient to foster subversive contaminations. On the contrary.

And it is no coincidence that, throughout the 1970s and early 1980s, the monetary question was not on the counterculture's agenda, except in purely ethical and/or anthropological terms (the myth of the return to the *good savage*,[2] especially under the influence of philosophical and anthropological philosophies).

The reason is simple. As long as monetary sovereignty is in the hands of the State, which acts according to the interests of the military-industrial apparatus, there is little to be done. The issuing monopoly represents too great a Moloch to allow one to even think of undermining it. Exodus, with the construction of a barter economy founded on solidarity, is the recognition of the industriousness and

---

2. The myth of the good savage dates back to romantic sentimentalism that developed in the seventeenth century and found its best synthesis with the Enlightenment thought of Rousseau. Cf. J. J. Rousseau, *Of The Social Contract and Other Political Writings* (London: Penguin Books, 2012).

creative activity of the members of the commune, and thus appears to be the only possible 'revolution'.

From this point of view, it is interesting to note that such a barter economy can only produce goods and services whose value is only use-value, at the very moment when monetary exchange is denied. There is therefore no nominal value that is determined at the very moment of exchange (monetary price), but the value of the product is determined based on the manner of its production. In fact, in the production of use-value what counts is the labour time required in the given production, as postulated by the classical labour-value theory. Work, or rather labour and social activity in the commons, is thus remunerated by being able to have free access to the consumer goods necessary for the social reproduction of human beings that nature allows:

> Labor is *not the source* of all wealth. *Nature* is just as much the source of use values (and it is surely of such that material wealth consists!) as labor, which itself is only the manifestation of a force of nature, human labor power.[3]

In fact, we are moving, from an economic point of view, into a context of primitive communism, where, with the abolition of money (and private property), those social conditions are also eliminated that decree

> that man, having no property other than his labour-power, must be, in all conditions of society, and of civilisation, the slave of those men who have made themselves owners of the material conditions of labour. He can work only with their permission, and therefore he can live only with their permission.[4]

In fact, when in the Marxist tradition we speak of the abolition of money in the future communist society (which should be achieved after the transitional phase of socialism), we refer not so much to the abolition of money as a means of payment and unit of account, but to the social role it plays as a credit-money. The abolition of money thus translates into the abolition of a private credit system and its nationalization. But

---

3. Cf. K. Marx, *Critique of the Gotha Programme* (1875), ch. 1, p. 1. Available online: https://www.marxists.org/archive/marx/works/1875/gotha/ch01.htm.

4. Cf. Marx, *Critique of the Gotha Programme*.

the question remains open, in the properly communist phase, of the extinction of the state and thus of any instrument of monetary issuance.

After the extermination of the American Indians,[5] as is well known, the only nation to have experimented on a large scale with the abolition of money in recent history was Cambodia in 1975–9 during the Khmer Rouge regime under Pol Pot. And the results were disastrous.[6]

5. The Native Americans or Indian nation have always rejected the use of money, which had no value for them, within community structures based on the solidarity-based distribution of the goods necessary for survival according to hierarchical rules handed down by tradition. This approach was well known to ordinary hippies, especially those who propagated a return to harmony with nature. Here are a few aphorisms of some Indian chiefs on the concept of wealth and, far ahead of their time, on the 'refusal of work'.

'Your people [referring to white men, ed.] look up to men because they are rich, because they have much land, many lodges, many women?' 'Yes' 'My people look up to me because I am poor. That is the difference.' (Sitting Bull: interview reported in *The Custer Myth: A Source Book of Custerania*, written and compiled by Colonel W. A. Graham (Harrisburg, PA: The Stackpole Co., 1953), 85–96. Available online: https://www.astonisher.com/archives/museum/sitting_bull_little_big_horn.html.)

'You white men pretend that we plough the land, that we cut the grass, that we get hay from it and sell it, so that we become rich. You white men know only work. My young men shall never work. Men who work cannot dream, and wisdom comes in dreams.' (Smohalla: quoted in A. F. Chamberlain, 'Wisdom of the North American Indian-in-Speech and Legend', in *American Antiquarian Society* (April 1913), 69.

6. The political programme of the Khmer Rouge, of Maoist derivation but with original elements, was extremely radical, perhaps the most radical that has existed within communist ideology: among other things, it envisaged isolation from foreign influences, complete statehood and the abolition of banks, finance and money. Policies were implemented to deport part of the population from the cities to the countryside on the basis of a forced cultivation plan that had tragic results: between famine, purges and massacres of ethnic and religious minorities, it is estimated that between 1.4 million (Amnesty International data) and 1.7 million deaths were recorded (Yale University data). It must, however, be remembered, in all fairness, that the Khmer Rouge justified the abolition of the money on the grounds that money was then waste paper in Cambodia and that the provisional measure was intended to help them make a fresh start and then re-establish a modern economy.

Directly introducing the abolition of money as an accounting means of payment is therefore only possible in small communities that have no exchange relations with the outside world: which, if it is possible for short periods of time, becomes unsustainable in the medium and long term. It follows that even small communities that have experimented with economic relations based on pure non-monetary barter exchanges (C-C: Merchandise against Merchandise) have sooner or later had to face the problem of defining a means of payment that would perform the functions of intermediary and fluidities of exchanges, thus moving to an C-M-C (Commodity-Money-Commodity) system. As the experience of the hippy communes themselves has shown, one cannot do so without a medium of exchange intermediation.

The issue then becomes not to abolish money, but which monetary instrument can be adopted or coined so as to be suitable for a solidarity-based economic model aimed at the production of use-value (the satisfaction of one's needs on the basis of one's possibilities[7]) and not exchange-value (profit).

To this end, the hippy communes are not able to provide an answer and above all are not able to make proposals equal to the economic crisis that from the early 1970s began to claim its first victims. On the contrary, it was precisely the crisis of the Fordist paradigm that irreversibly marked the decline of the communes' experiences of alternative and primitive economics, at the very moment when scarcity contrasted with the previous abundance of the 1960s.

The collapse of Bretton Woods and the transition to immaterial money

The history of money is connected to the history of mankind. Long ago, until the formation of nation states in the 1500s in Europe, the prevailing form of money was commodity money. The value of the money is contained in the body of the coin itself. Its metallic (i.e. physical, be

---

7. The reference is obviously to K. Marx: 'From each according to his/her ability, to each according to his/her need', in Marx, *Critique of the Gotha Programme*. Available online: https://www.marxists.org/archive/marx/works/1875/gotha/index.htm. This phrase, made famous by Marx, is derives from the Acts of the Apostles (cf. Acts 4:35).

it copper, bronze, silver or gold) form (weight) indicates its value. Thus, an exchange between equivalents in value takes place. A metre of cloth that, let us suppose, has a value of 10 grams of gold, is directly exchanged for a coin that contains 10 grams of gold. From this point of view, the exchange of money implies a rival and solvent exchange. That specific 10-gram coin can only be used for that exchange, in a quid pro quo relationship, commodity (cloth) versus commodity (metal-gold). The coin is thus a commodity (good) like any other.

According to Herodotus,[8] the Lydians were the first people to introduce the use of gold and silver coins and the first to establish 'shops' for retailing in permanent locations. At the very moment that metallic money became widespread as a means of payment and became a unit of account for economic exchange (a unit for measuring value), it also became an expression of power. It was in fact he who issued the currency (the sovereign) who determined its value and expressed economic command.

In this phase of history (Euro-Mediterranean), the currency-commodity implies a proprietary structure (like all commodities). Ownership is expressed in the issuing monopoly (the sovereign). Seigniorage rights are not yet acted upon. It will be with the Roman Empire, first with Nero and then with Septimius Severus, that the value of money (aureus and denarius, in gold and silver respectively) will tend no longer to correspond exactly to the quantity of precious metal used. Thus seigniorage rights arose.

But it was only with the formation of the European nation-states and the technological paradigm shift at the turn of the fifteenth to sixteenth centuries that the total decoupling between the declared value of the money and the quantity of the precious metal it contained took place.

The money-issuing monopoly then takes the form of a supra-individual right and money becomes an extra-market variable, controlled institutionally and not by market dynamics. Once guaranteed by the state role, which operates not as a market agent but above it, money also begins to perform the function of a store of value and patrimonial measure. This phase shift is, not coincidentally, accompanied by a change in the form of money. From metallic money, predominantly

---

8. Cf. Herodotus, *The Histories*, vol. I, fr. 94. See also M. Cowell and K. Hyne, 'Scientific Examination of the Lydian Precious Metal Coinages', in A. Ramage and P. Craddock (eds), *King Croesus' Gold: Excavations at Sardis and the History of Gold Refining* (Cambridge, MA: Harvard University Press, 2000), 169–74.

based on gold, we move to paper money: this means that the monetary medium no longer incorporates the very value it declares. As we have recalled, the economic exchange 'value for quantity' had always existed as an exchange of pure and direct equivalents in commodities, that is, a certain amount of gold for a certain amount of commodities. It is no coincidence that most of the names of currencies in force today, or until recently, are etymologically derived from units of weight (pounds in Britain, pesetas in Spain, lira – from libra – in many countries). With the guarantee of state (hence institutional and extra-private market) governance, economic exchange is increasingly becoming materially characterized as an exchange between a piece of paper, whose intrinsic value is little, and a certain amount of commodity. But this piece of paper – the paper money or banknote – is guaranteed by a higher political power that obliges acceptance (trust) and guarantees the virtual value on it. This passage generates, through the increasingly important role of the Central Bank, the possibility of creating a monetary base under monopoly conditions (seigniorage).

Thus, with the industrial revolution and, in the twentieth century, with the Bretton Woods Conference, we see the gradual abandonment of monetary systems based on precious metals and the convertibility of coins into precious metals. The growth of economic exchange, caused by the spread of the capitalist system of production, forced the use of currencies whose supply was not constrained by the limited availability of precious metals. Moreover, the emergence of certain currencies, increasingly widespread and accepted in international trade, made the use of precious metals to regulate such trade obsolete. Finally, the emergence of the banknote and other forms of payment unencumbered by the use of precious metals is explained by the convenience of payment systems that do not require the transfer of large quantities of heavy precious metals.

Today, after the end of Bretton Woods, we are witnessing the complete dematerialization of money. Its value, conventionally fixed in 1944 at Bretton Woods at the ratio of $35 per ounce of gold, has decayed. From 'commodity' money and 'gold' money we pass to money as a 'pure sign' (Marx), a passage that, thanks to the process of financialization, has de facto reduced the weight of seigniorage rights and also the possibility for Central Banks to fully control the money supply in circulation and the credit and financial multiplier that follows.

Money thus tends to dematerialize completely. Today, money is no longer a commodity or a good. There is no longer a unit for measuring the value of money, like the metre for length or the kilogram for weight. Irrespective of the fact that issuing monopolies and seigniorage rights still exist, irrespective of the ownership structure, as no longer a commodity, money cannot even be called a common good. With the end of the Bretton Woods agreements, the value of money is no longer determined by who issues it. Monetary sovereignty (whether national or supranational), the governance of which is the task of the Central Bank, loses more and more meaning.

And it is in this context, with the disappearance of effective monetary authority (although the central role of Central Banks remains), that new perspectives open up for thinking and imagining alternative monetary systems.

The de-institutionalization of money

What does the expression 'the disappearance of the Central Banks' authority to control money' mean in concrete terms?

It means that Central Banks are no longer the only institutions that can 'create' money. Other economic actors, operating within the economic market, are now able to alter the money supply.

With the transition from Taylorist-Fordist capitalism to financialized bio-cognitive capitalism, the main function of money changes. The credit function, typical of an M-C-M system, where investment activity in the production of goods requires monetary anticipation and the indebtedness of economic actors (be they private enterprises or the State), leaves more and more room for finance money (financial production economy). Finance money, not by chance, coincides with the total dematerialization of money, being *pure sign money*.

It is important to emphasize that this shift from credit-money to finance-money implies a change in monetary governance: the former was and still is issued under the control of monetary institutions (Central Banks), whereas the latter depends on the dynamics of the financial market.

Here, then, are new economic subjects that enter the mechanism of money creation, but as we shall see, if the financial markets, in the manner we shall now explain, are the main actors in this process, they are not the only ones.

Until the crisis of Fordism, in fact, the institution of the Central Bank had the task of exercising direct and precise control over the quantity of money (M1) issued by the national mints (*fiat money*). But over 90 per cent of the money supply is now provided by private banks and financial investors, in the form of loans or speculative activities, over whose share the Central Bank has only very indirect and limited control. This means that although the Central Bank can unilaterally and autonomously set interest rates and impose reserve requirements on banks, the amount of money in circulation is less controllable by the Central Bank itself. In a capitalist system based on a financial economy of production, the quantity of money is endogenously determined by the level of economic activity and by the evolution of the financial conventions (in Keynesian terms) that govern the international financial market.[9] The Central Bank can only try to increase or decrease the supply of money in circulation (in any case a minimal share of the total), but nothing more, chasing and pandering to the dynamics of the financial indices themselves. This possibility is now further reduced by the new role played by the financial markets in the process of financing investment activity, through capital gains and the creation of highly liquid securities (defined as *near money*).

Paradoxically, it follows that Central Banks' discretionary powers are reduced the more they themselves have become politically autonomous institutions. As a consequence, the Central Bank's powers of control and supervision over the banking sector and, through interest rate changes, over the entire economic system are increasingly functional to the dynamics at work in the financial markets and increasingly dependent on the oligarchies that dominate them.

This means that, in bio-cognitive capitalism, money and the determination of its value are no longer under the control of the Central Bank. At the very moment that money is pure sign it escapes any public control. Money thus loses its status as a 'good of public control'. Its value is determined from time to time by the operation of speculative activities on the financial markets. Its functions as means of payment and unit of account (measure of value), as well as store of value and means of financing accumulation/development, become

9. The concept of 'financial convention' goes back to J. M. Keynes: see J. M. Keynes, *General Theory of Employment, Interest and Money* (London: Macmillan, 1936), especially ch. XII. A financial convention is generated when the expectations of the main stock exchange operators, usually the large multinational finance corporations, operate jointly upwards (buying) or downwards (selling) on certain financial securities (public or private) in order to condition the dynamics of the indices of the main stock exchanges. See also footnote 54 of previous chapter.

out of control. As its quantity and mode of circulation are determined by the conventions that dominate increasingly concentrated financial markets, money becomes hostage to the expectations that the oligarchy (or rather, the dictatorship of the oligarchy[10]) of the financial markets is able to exert.

Today, we can say that financial money creation is the expression of the libertarian communism of capital.[11] This is confirmed by the dependence of monetary policy on financial dynamics.

Let us remember this expression! It indicates the ability of those who manage large investment and pension funds to oppose the control of the Central Bank, to perform an anti-state function. This may appear in the eyes of those who see the presence of the state as one of the evils

10. Let us remember that just over a dozen large multinational finance corporations control, without being their direct owners, portfolios of financial assets amounting to some 65–70 per cent of total global financial transactions. In the US, three banks (Goldman Sachs, JPMorgan Chase, Citibank National) held 78 per cent of the derivatives traded in the country as at 31 December 2002. Cf. https://www.occ.gov/publications-and-resources/publications/quarterly-report-on-bank-trading-and-derivatives-activities/files/pub-derivatives-quarterly-qtr4-2022.pdf.

11. This expression is taken up by C. Marazzi: cf. C. Marazzi, *Il comunismo del capitale* (Verona: Ombre Corte, 2015). See also, in English, C. Marazzi, *The Violence of Financial Capitalism* (Cambridge, MA: Semiotext(e), MIT Press, 2011). The term 'communism of capital' was, however, coined in advance by Toni Negri within the theoretical analysis of Italian *operaismo* (*workerism*) at the end of the 1960s, at the conference in Padua in 1967, the proceedings of which were later published in the collected volume (edited by S. Bologna, G. P. Rawick, M. Gobbini, A. Negri, L. Ferrari Bravo and F. Gambino), *Operai e Stato* (Milan: Feltrinelli, 1972). In particular, see Toni Negri's essay, 'John M. Keynes and the Capitalist Theory of the State in '29', p. 100, where we read: 'The communism of capital will be able to absorb every value in its movement, to represent fully the social reason for development: it will never be able to make its own that particular worker's hatred of exploitation, uncontainable, at every level of equilibrium, because it is a project for the destruction of the capitalist mode of production' (my translation). In this text, Negri refers to the 'communism of capital' by analysing the role of Keynesian welfare policies that developed after the Second World War. Marazzi, on the other hand, refers to the illusory role of financial markets in individually creating wealth for all ('enrichez vous').

of eradicating a positive factor, which goes against a libertarian logic, typical of much of North American political thought. But it must also be recognized that in this way money becomes an expression of financial bio-power, the outcome of the expropriation of the common, as a new form of labour exploitation in bio-cognitive capitalism.

Micro-trading and complementary and/or alternative currencies

The information technology revolution, the new linguistic technologies, the development of algorithms and digital communication began to involve the world of monetary relations, their morphology, as early as the late 1980s. Cyber and digital technology, far from representing an elsewhere, enters powerfully into the scene of social or, better, financial innovation.

The monopoly of issuance can be broken. Two philosophies oppose each other. We have already observed how the process of financialization alludes to the possibility of democratizing access to money. The expansion of financial markets in the second half of the 1980s opens up the illusion of new spaces of monetary agility. The latter moves in two directions, mutually complementary but also competitive: firstly, the possibility for all and sundry to access financial wealth through access to financial speculation using the new information technologies that allow the development of so-*called micro-trading*,[12] and secondly, the development of alternative and complementary forms of payment to the 'official' ones.

It is precisely the new digital technologies, born out of the counterculture of the 1970s, that allow free access to financial activity. The barriers to entry to the financial markets, imposed by financial companies and credit banks, begin to be relaxed: the obligation to use a financial intermediary, to pay the relevant commissions, is increasingly bypassed by the spread of software programs that allow anyone to trade securities on the financial markets without limits and controls. Financial markets are thus the only ones that allow free access to all and sundry. From this point of view, they can be represented as free and highly competitive markets.

12. L. Black and H. Todd, *The Microtrading Revolution: An Insiders Guide to SOES/ECN Trading*, 1st edn (New York: Microtrade Inc., 1998). For the Italian debate, cf. A. Fumagalli (ed.), *Finanza fai da te* (Rome: Derive Approdi, 2001).

Open finance as open source: thanks to new digital technologies. From this perspective, the democratization of financial markets goes hand in hand with the democratization of knowledge, against all financial intermediation and intellectual property rights.

The cyber revolution, the cyber counterculture, and the underground it develops, is thus able to challenge the strong powers of finance and multinational industry in a way that the hippy counterculture of the 1960s had never been able to do.

In the course of the 1980s and, above all, in the course of the 1990s, 'do-it-yourself finance' became more and more important, without, however, ever undermining the oligopolistic power of the large multinationals of finance. If anything, it participates in the widening of financial markets, favouring, albeit to a limited extent, the growth of share indices, which in the USA in the 1990s, up to March 2000, reached the highest values and, above all, a period of more or less uninterrupted growth ever recorded (seven years) in the history of global stock exchanges.

Micro traders in the US trade more on the Nasdaq (the stock market index of technology stocks) than on the Dow Jones (the general index of the US stock market). They are self-employed. We could call them Generation III self-employed workers,[13] to distinguish them from Generation II self-employed workers,[14] who essentially work in business services. Generation III self-employed workers, on the other hand, are workers who are not employed and who work on their own in cognitive-communication-intensive activities along the lines of freelancers.

Micro traders, in fact, work from home, via modem, but cannot be defined as teleworkers because they are not employed by any financial company. They have very different characteristics from financial promoters (who earn commissions on financial packages they manage to place to customers on behalf of some financial company). Instead, the activity that the micro trader carries out is purely speculative, that

13. A. Fumagalli, 'Le trasformazioni del lavoro autonomo tra crisi e precarietà: il lavoro autonomo di III generazione', in *Quaderni di ricerca sull'artigianato* 2 (2015): 228–56.

14. Cfr. S. Bologna and A. Fumagalli (eds), *I lavoratori autonomi di II generazione. Scenari del postfordismo in Italia* (Milano: Feltrinelli, 1997). In English, see S. Rapelli, 'European I-Pros: A Study. Professional Contractors Group (PCG)', 2012. Available online: http://rapelli.free.fr/documents/rapelli _pcg_en.pdf.

is, he or she derives his or her earnings from the difference in value of securities between the moment of sale and the moment of purchase. These are transactions that have a very limited duration, based on the logical sequence: money – buying and selling securities – money surplus, which takes place in the very short term.

The weight of micro trading in the US is no more than 10–12 per cent, while the use of software programs for buying and selling securities has spread rapidly. Today, for example, it is estimated that in the US more than 70 per cent of stock purchases by financial traders take place with *high-frequency trading* (HFT),[15] and the Bank of England estimates this figure to be 40 per cent for Europe.

One can conclude that, as in the field of open source, technological innovation alludes to greater spaces of freedom, but then in the concrete reality of the facts is susceptible to the intensification of capitalist capture and subsumption processes.

It is not surprising, therefore, that the weight of the financial markets has greatly increased with the financialization of the economy and the liberalization of the capital market, the outcome of a precise liberalist political choice during the 1980s. If the Gross Domestic Product of the entire world in 2010 was 74 trillion dollars, finance surpasses it: the world bond market is worth 95 trillion dollars, stock exchanges around the world 50, derivatives 466 (eight times more than real wealth). All this is well known, but what we often forget to point out is that this process, in addition to shifting the focus of capitalist valorization from material to immaterial production and from exploitation by manual labour alone to exploitation by cognitive labour alone, has given rise to a new 'original accumulation', which, like all original accumulations, is characterized by a high degree of concentration.

In the banking market, from 1980 to 2005 (before the 2007–8 financial crisis) there were about 11,500 mergers, an average of 440 per year, reducing the number of banks to less than 7,500 (Federal Reserve data). As of the first quarter of 2011, five investment companies (i.e. Securities Dealers, SIMs) – JPMorgan, Bank of America, Citibank, Goldman Sachs, HSBC USA, and five banks – Deutsche Bank, UBS, Credit Suisse, Citigroup, BNP Paribas) controlled more than 90 per cent of the total derivative securities (OCC data, Office of Comptroller of the Currency).[16]

15. Cf. https://en.wikipedia.org/wiki/High-frequency_trading.

16. In the US at 31 December 2022, three banks (Goldman Sachs, JPMorgan Chase, Citibank National) held 78% of the derivatives traded in the country.

In the stock market, merger and acquisition strategies have substantially reduced the number of listed companies. As of today, the top ten companies with the largest market capitalization, 0.12 per cent of the 7,800 registered companies, hold 41 per cent of the total value, 47 per cent of the revenues and 55 per cent of the registered capital gains.

From these data, we can deduce that, in reality, financial markets are not something impartial and neutral, but are the expression of a precise hierarchy: far from being competitive, they conceal a pyramid, which sees, at the top, a few financial operators capable of controlling over 65 per cent of global financial flows and, at the bottom, a myriad of small savers and financial operators who perform a passive function (including micro trading). This market structure allows a few companies (in particular the ten mentioned above) to direct and condition market dynamics. In other words, define the dominant financial conventions. Moreover, the rating companies (often colluding with the financial companies themselves) instrumentally ratify the oligarchic decisions that are taken from time to time.

When we read statements such as 'it is the markets that are asking for it', 'it is the judgement of the markets' and comments of this kind, we must realize that these so-called markets, ideologically presented as metaphysical, neutral and therefore objective entities, are nothing more than the expression of a specific power.

True political governance no longer lies in political institutions, but in the financial hierarchy, dictated by the outcomes of financial speculation.

The libertarian communism of capital is formally characterized by free access, but in reality favours processes of concentration in the control and management of increasingly large financial portfolios.

In the face of such a process of financial concentration, the possibility of micro trading playing an anti-systemic role is practically nil. Rather, its function, as is often the case with technological innovations and social conflicts that push the hands of history forward, is to press capitalism towards adjustments that are perhaps ameliorative, but certainly not capable of modifying the logic of exploitation of man over man and repression of freedom of choice that lies at its origin.

Cf. https://www.occ.gov/publications-and-resources/publications/quarterly-report-on-bank-trading-and-derivatives-activities/files/pub-derivatives-quarterly-qtr4-2022.pdf.

In the 2000s, at the threshold of the new millennium, the illusion that micro trading could constitute a significant experience capable of conditioning the dynamics of the financial markets was set forever. Today, it remains alive as an advertising manifesto of the hypothesis of getting rich individually, without any aura of alternative.

But the cyber underground does not stand idle. Increasingly sophisticated technologies make it possible to explore lesser-known territories. Cyberspace has no boundaries, nor does the mathematics of complex numbers and chaos theory.

Nothing new, conceptually speaking, is discovered. At this point, the notion of an algorithm is central. An algorithm is a procedure that solves a given problem through a finite number of elementary steps. The term is derived from the Latin transcription of the name of the Persian mathematician al-Khwarizmi, who is considered to be one of the first authors to have referred to this concept. The algorithm is a fundamental concept in computer science, first of all because it is the basis of the theoretical notion of computability: a problem is computable when it can be solved by an algorithm. Furthermore, the algorithm is also a pivotal concept in the programming phase of software development.

But what one discovers is the possibility of putting into practice, here and now, the data processing opportunities that new technologies allow, through the creation of open source and peer-to-peer software capable of modelling new modes of monetary exchange.

This opens up new perspectives, typically more underground, not so much aimed at modifying from within the existing monetary command devices modelled on the capitalist hierarchy, but rather at creating spaces for autonomous action.

The recent development of complementary currencies was the logical consequence. Complementary currencies have reason to exist as long as they operate in an autonomous space. This space is not only a virtual space – such as the one created by the internet – but also has a concrete impact within the existing economic system.

There is an immediate reference to the concept of TAZ (Temporary Autonomous Zone), introduced in *T.A.Z.: The Temporary Autonomous Zone, Ontological Anarchy, Poetic Terrorism*, by Hakim Bey in 1991.[17] The book describes the socio-political tactic of temporarily creating self-managed spaces in order to circumvent the formal structures and

17. Cf. H. Bey (P. L. Wilson), *T.A.Z.: The Temporary Autonomous Zone* (New York: Autonomedia, 1991).

institutions imposed by social control, re-proposing the strategy of the libertarian exodus to fight the enemy from the outside. The exodus propagated by Hakim Bey is, however, unlike the hippy counterculture, a subjective mental exodus, in order to create anti-institutional social relations by focusing on the present and freeing one's mind from the mechanisms that have been imposed on it. Bey's essay takes as its reference point the post-Gauchist anarchy, the hacker movement and also much of the techno-rave and cyberpunk subcultures that have developed since the 1990s.

The concept of the autonomous zone, no longer on the level of human subjectivity/surplus but on that of economic relations, is taken up by the similar concept of FAZ, or Financial Autonomous Zone. In the words of Domenico De Simone and Marco Giustini, who more than others in Italy have promoted this concept, the FAZ defines:

> an alternative economic system based on abundance instead of scarcity. The objective of the FAZ is to create communities between subjects that share values, economic and social relations, and productive activities, equipping them with a legal instrument that can be traced back to a 'complementary currency'. The FAZ is a concrete proposal for a structural and sustainable economic change through an innovative model of socio-productive aggregation, based on participation, that facilitates both the creation of wealth and its social redistribution, guaranteeing the support, protection and development of the local economy, the protection of the economically weaker segments of the local population, and the increase in the provision of public utility services, without generating debt. In essence, by joining the FAZ, companies, associations, institutions and individuals will have the opportunity to manage their economic and social relations using the peculiar tools that the FAZ will make available to them: a virtual currency to be used within the FAZ, interest-free loans, citizenship income distributed periodically and equally to all participants according to the wealth produced within the FAZ itself.[18]

18. Cf. D. De Simone and M. Giustini, 'FAZ. Financial Autonomous Zone', in E. Braga and A. Fumagalli (eds), *La moneta del comune. La sfida dell'istituzione finanziaria del comune* (Rome: Derive Approdi – Alfabeta, 2015), 99.

The FAZ is based on an idea of an economic system that is founded on abundance rather than scarcity. This abundance derives from the fact that, in an economy increasingly founded on the valorization of immaterial production to the detriment of material production, the productive factors that are the most important are knowledge and space – whose meaning has more to do with relational and network activity than defined in geographical-territorial terms. These two inputs are abundant by definition, to the point of being able to prefigure a post-scarcity economy.

These arguments are based on the pioneering contribution of Richard Stallman[19] and later Cory Doctorow,[20] according to whom a 'post-scarcity economy' is a system of management and allocation of resources that are always sufficient to meet the perceived needs of individuals. However, the economy as we know it, the 'scarcity economy', is a system in which there is an efficient allocation of resources that are by definition scarce, that is, always less than the perceived needs of individuals.[21]

And it is precisely on the basis of the axiom that bio-cognitive capitalism, drawing its sap directly from human life and being as abundant as human life is widespread, is characterized by 'non-scarcity', that it is possible to create autonomous spaces of social and economic freedom (of TAZs capable of generating spaces of financial autonomy, hence FAZs).

19. See R. Stallman, 'GNU Manifesto', 1985. Available online: https://www.gnu.org/gnu/manifesto.en.html. The GNU Manifesto was written by Richard Stallman at the beginning of the GNU project, in 1985, to solicit help in developing the GNU system. Some of the text comes from an earlier announcement in 1983. Until 1987 the manifesto was slightly updated to reflect developments, but since that time the best choice seems to be to leave it unchanged.

20. Cf. C. Doctorow, *Down and Out in the Magic Kingdom* (New York: Tor Books, 2003).

21. The traditional definition of economics, which is found in all mainstream Political Economy textbooks studied in the world, is still that of Lionel Robbins: 'Economics is the science which studies human behavior as a relationship between ends and scares means which have alternative uses.' Cf. L. Robbins, *The Nature and Significance of Economic Science*, 2nd edn (London: Macmillan, 1935), 16.

The concept of the FAZ is particularly dear to the cyberpunk and anarchist tradition, although it has had less luck than the concept of the TAZ. However, it is important because it creates the basis for the development in the first decade of the new millennium for the spread of complementary currency systems.

Initially, the first complementary currencies have the status of commodity currencies, that is, they must somehow be linked to a physical-material unit of measure. And as in the barter economy, the measure is the time of human activity, measured in hours.

In 1991, the first attempt to create an alternative monetary circuit was developed: the Ithaca Hours.[22]

The Ithaca Hour is a local currency used in Ithaca, New York, that has inspired other similar systems in various locations in the United States. An Ithaca Hour has a value of US$10 and is generally recommended to be used as payment for an hour's work, although this value may be negotiable.

The connection to time is immediate and it is in fact a time bank's monetary accounting structure. It follows that this currency predominantly performs functions as a means of payment and unit of account, even within the exchange on the labour market, but without performing functions as a store of value (as a function of possible speculative activity), or as money-credit (it has no interest rate). These functions are guaranteed by the fact that the Ithaca Hour cannot be exchanged for dollars. We therefore move in a parallel economy where there is no accumulation, within an C-M-C (Commodity-Money-Commodity) scheme, aimed at the simple reproduction of the economic system.

However, this does not mean that there cannot also be beneficial effects for the entire economic system.

The Ithaca Hour expands the local money supply promotes and expands local commerce, it can allow for an increase in the local minimum wage to $10.00, benefiting not only workers but also businesses, it increases local demand, handicrafts and locally grown organic food. The Ithaca Hour can encourage new businesses and jobs as well as reduce dependence on imports and transportation fuels and subsidize non-profit organisations in the community.[23]

22. Cf. https://en.wikipedia.org/wiki/Ithaca_Hours

23. On the official website (http://www.ithacahours.com) you can read: 'HOURS expand the local money supply. HOURS promote and expand

The Ithaca Hour was invented and founded by Paul Glover in 1991 and until 1996 the banknotes were printed directly at his home. From that year on, the system had an advisory board and a board of directors called the 'Barter Potluck'.[24] Glower and co.'s initial assumption was that economic exchanges should be based on harmony rather than competition of Hobbesian memory (*homo hominis lupus*). In an interview, Glover stated that 'there is a movement spreading, called the ecological economy and Ithaca Hours is part of this cosmos'. This confirms that an underlying principle of the local currency movement is to create 'fair trade', with the intention of minimizing conflict and exploitation of both people and natural resources.[25]

It is important to note that the ideology of Ithaca Hours is closely linked to the counterculture of the 1970s, with the difference that the new experimentation does not take place outside the dominant economic reality but within it, with the intention of trying to contaminate it.

The Ithaca Hours system is an example of what in those years and in the following years tended to spread, especially in Anglo-Saxon countries: the LETS (Local Exchange Trading Systems),[26] that is, conventions between economic actors to generate on a fiduciary basis exchange relations based on the use value of goods. That is, they are non-profit agencies with solidarity objectives, aimed at experimenting, researching new sustainable development models for local and community economies through the use of complementary currencies.

As of 2011, these agencies, scattered around the world, organize more than 1,500 groups in thirty-nine countries with the aim of training and informing individuals and associations on practical and ethical guidelines on how to organize their local LETS node.

local shopping, with an endless multiplier. HOURS double the local minimum wage to $10.00, benefitting not only workers but businesses as well, who find new and loyal customers. HOURS enable shoppers to afford premium prices for locally-crafted goods and for locally-grown organic food. HOURS help start new businesses and jobs. HOURS reduce dependence on imports and transport fuels. HOURS make grants to nonprofit community organizations. HOURS make zero-interest loans. HOURS stimulate community pride.'

24. Cf. E. Nieves, 'Our Towns; Ithaca Hours: Pocket Money For Everyman', *New York Times*, 21 January 1996.

25. Cf. https://en.wikipedia.org/wiki/Ithaca_Hours.

26. Cf. http://www.lets-linkup.com/.

The first node was created in Great Britain in 1991 by Liz Shepard and soon the LETS system became widespread, especially in Great Britain. But it was not until the following decade that the phenomenon of complementary currencies exploded, when the development of technology and algorithms made it possible to model a currency that was, to all intents and purposes, digital, and thus totally dematerialized and disengaged from a temporal unit of measurement, as the local currencies linked to the LETS circuit were anyway.

Cryptocurrencies and capital algorithms

It is with the new millennium that the encounter between cyberculture, hacker activity and complementary currencies takes place: the so-called cryptocurrencies are born, which present themselves, precisely because of their cultural backgrounds, as alternative currencies.

The spectrum of alternative currencies is widening.

In a recent essay, Marco Sachy aka Radium proposes a taxonomy of unconventional and complementary currencies and payment systems:

- Local exchange circuits: LETS (Local Exchange Trading Schemes mainly in English-speaking countries) and LOVE (Local Value Exchange in Japan).
- Local currencies: 'Transition Currencies', e.g. the Transition Pounds in the UK (Bristol Pound: http://bit.ly/1tu7vfO), local currencies designed to insulate (rather than 'isolate') a local economy from financial disturbances from outside.
- Counter-cyclical Business-to-business (B2B) currencies, for example the Commercial Credit Circuit, or C3, in which Uruguayan businesses use invoice payments as currency within the small business circuit (http://bit.ly/1Ew87Kq). An example from the world of crypto-currencies is the Freicoin, a negative rate Bitcoin (https://freico.in) [in Italy, the best-known example is Sardex, ed.].
- Currency with exclusively social purposes: an example is the Chiemgauer, a regional currency issued in Bavaria to support local businesses and charities (https://en.wikipedia.org/wiki/Chiemgauer).
- Corporate currencies: from supermarket points to flight miles.[27]

27. Cf. M. Sachy aka Radium, 'Freecoin: la cripto-blockchain come bene comune', in Braga and Fumagalli (eds), *La moneta del comune*, 144.

Among cryptocurrencies, the best-known example is Bitcoin (BTC). It originated as a currency – produced by peer-to-peer networks in a decentralized and anonymous manner – to be used for the main function of currency, that is, as a medium of exchange. Since its inception some five years ago, however, its value has been defined by its conversion ratio with the US dollar, to which other currencies such as the Euro, British Pound, Russian Ruble and Chinese Yuan have been added over time. The BTC therefore also falls under the dollar index system even though, as it has no legal value, no exchange with the aforementioned currencies is recognized and implemented.

Regarding its diffusion as a means of payment, since its birth, an increasing number of businesses – mostly but not only e-commerce – have accepted it in transactions, always pegging the price of goods and services to their value in dollars, still the international reference currency. As is well known, the BTC is also the most widespread means of payment on the net for illegal transactions that take place in the so-called deep web where anonymity and the (apparent) non-traceability of the actors in transactions are considered to be added value.

Until about four years ago, the value of the BTC was US$9, barely enough to cover the costs necessary for its generation by those who with their computers decided to enter the peer-to-peer network necessary for the production or, as they say, 'mining' of the string/currency.

The costs were related to the setting up of a computer capable of high computing capacity and the (not insignificant) costs of electricity.

Two characteristics inherent in the BTC algorithm (and common to all cryptocurrencies) made its investment even more risky: the finite number of extractable strings – a maximum of 21 million for BTC – and the progressive increase in the difficulty of extracting 'strings', in relation to the total number extracted and the overall quantity and processing capacity progressively expressed by the network. This, at the same time, implied that, as the 21 million strings extracted approached, the value of the BTC would necessarily increase, provided, of course, that it was actually and effectively disseminated as a means of payment. Otherwise, at the end, only alphanumeric strings would remain.

The BTC and the other numerous currencies born in its emulation are simply encrypted files, that is, alphanumeric sequences (numbers and letters) generated by computers – following the execution and resolution of a certain algorithm – placed within a peer-to-peer network. The algorithm is specific to each 'coin'. There are also 'suites' for the creation of 'do-it-yourself' coins: algorithms that generate strings.

The idea itself is not new; already national governmental and banking institutions have, for some time, gone down the path of attributing monetary value to artificially created sequences of numbers based on the dynamics of state, corporate and personal debt/credit. The algorithm is obviously different; in this context, its function is fulfilled by the banks' reserve percentages, interest rates and the simple decision to generate money.

In the case of cryptocurrencies, the main novelty lies in the substitution of the decision-making subject: no longer are economic institutions democratically deputed to manage monetary and financial policy, but rather the multitude of individuals who decide to produce or 'extract' the 'strings' with their networked computers, and the multitude of individuals who decide (trustingly) to recognize monetary value in those generated strings.

In a machinic-algorithmic age such as the one in which we live, it should come as no surprise that money is no longer printed but generated, and that trust is no longer placed in human action but in the formal correctness of an algorithm executed by machines and/or the decisions of techno-financial elites.

This is the aspect that provides an aura of alternativeness to cryptocurrencies.

It is precisely the distrust of ethical and political action that underlies their emergence. The dependence of traditional currencies on institutional subjects whose decisions are no longer made to protect the individual and his freedom has prompted the creators of cryptocurrencies and their main proponents to seek such protection in the impartial action of machines.

This overturns the idea that machines are the instrument for the repression of individual freedoms, acted upon by institutional power structures functioning to perpetuate the domination of human beings over human beings.

Cybernetic development, on the other hand, now allows a level of impartiality of the machine that can make the utopia of an electronic democracy capable of respecting individual subjectivities – so dear to anarcho-capitalist thought – finally come true.

According to this utopia, even the democratic process could – indeed, should – be replaced by algorithmic decisions executed impartially by computers.

Justice is impartiality, and politics, which no longer appears able to implement it, must be replaced by machines whose behaviour is not conditioned by particularism of any kind. The political experiments of so-called 'electronic democracy' are also heading in this direction, although they do not envisage the complete substitution – as yet – of 'data processing' for collective decision-making.

It is a pity, however, that politics – in its meaning oriented towards social equity – is, on the contrary, precisely a choice of 'partiality' and that social justice can only be determined by the taking of 'partisan' decisions, that is, favouring the reduction of the disadvantageous conditions in which the many find themselves in relation to the (increasingly richer) few.

Instead of changing politics, politics is eliminated and we rely on an 'electronic regulator' in solving the problems of collective coexistence, which are traced back to the greater or lesser freedom of the individual.[28] From this perspective, the currency created by algorithms risks being conceived as de facto neutral to the system of wealth production and distribution.

But the BTC experience goes in another direction. At the time when BTC began to spread about fourteen years ago, almost marking the end of the 'taboo on money',[29] articles in the specialized press had attracted the attention of an ever-growing public, leading on the one hand to an increase in the number of miners and on the other hand to an increase in the number of establishments accepting it as a means of payment.

Being a currency subject to scarcity and being flexible in its quotation in dollars, as its use spreads, the BTC becomes an object of speculative exchange. As a currency with the function of a means of payment and unit of account, it becomes a store of value, awaiting its future appreciation.[30]

Thus, some brokerage firms also specialize in financial trading, allowing BTC to be 'traded' on a par with any currency on the Forex market, with the possibility of leverage. Forex is known to be the most 'liquid', high-volume and speculative market in existence.

28. Cf. A. Fumagalli and G. Giannelli, 'Il fenomeno Bitcoin: moneta alternativa o moneta speculativa?', 17 December 2013. Available online: http://effimera.org/il-fenomeno-bitcoin-moneta-alternativa-o-moneta-speculativa-gianluca-giannelli-e-andrea-fumagalli/.

29. Cf. D. Roio aka Jaromil, 'Bitcoin, the End of the Taboo on Money', 2013. Available online: http://median.newmediacaucus.org/isea2012-machine-wilderness/bitcom-the-end-of-the-taboo-on-money/.

30. In 2010, one could buy a whole bitcoin token for about US$0.09, while today its value is around US$26,000.

Moreover, there is no shortage of investment companies ready to launch specific derivatives on BTC that can insure holders or producers/dealers against future fluctuations in its value, similar to what happens with commodities or agricultural and or food products.

Likewise, other brokers inaugurate specific 'CFD/BTC' ('contract for difference' on BTC), leveraged financial instruments, tradable in the 'OTC' (over the counter) financial circuit.

Bitcoin enters its dimension as a speculative investment asset, thus moving from the computer 'bit', which had characterized its past, to the financial 'tick' that represents its present.[31]

The BTC case is paradigmatic of the possible parable of cryptocurrencies when thrown to the mercy of financial speculative markets, and it is no coincidence that it produces new followers.

Among other examples, we refer to the new cryptocurrency named Ripple. The reason is simple. In English, Ripple means ripple. It is also the title of a well-known song by the Grateful Dead, written by Robert Hunter and set to music by Jerry Garcia, whose lyrics, sentimental in nature, refer to a virtual world where affection constitutes a kind of cornucopia of abundance.

Now, there is no official statement linking the name of the digital money with the Grateful Dead song, although there are symbolic references. However, we believe there is an analogy, since the project originated in California in anarcho-capitalist circles.

Ripple is actually something more complex than Bitcoin. It is a digital platform that includes a digital money, namely Ripple: a kind of architecture to manage transactions in real currencies. It was built by the startup OpenCoin, which plans to give away shares in the virtual coinage in order to expand its spread.

The founders of OpenCoin are well-known faces in the open-source community. The CEO is Chris Larsen[32] and he launched, among other things, the Prosper peer-to-peer lending project. Jed McCaleb has the role of chief technology officer: he built the eDonkey peer-to-peer network for file sharing and launched Mt. Gox. Ripple is open

---

31. The trading *tick* is the minimum variation between two prices that can be placed on the market and represents the fraction of a predefined unit of the currency in which the security is traded. E.g. EU/USD exchange rate 1.09101 (18 August 2023) – the 'tick' is the fifth digit after the decimal point. Cf. Fumagalli and Giannelli, 'Il fenomeno Bitcoin'.

32. Cf. https://en.wikipedia.org/wiki/Chris_Larsen.

source like Bitcoin: it means that a community of software developers can make changes and share them according to the rules of the user licences. Which confirms the cyberculture background of its inventors.

Ripple is a decentralized platform: it uses a network of databases distributed in different geographical locations around the world but with headquarters in San Francisco. Unlike Bitcoin, it has ledgers (called Ledgers) to track exchanges that help complete transactions within seconds, whereas Bitcoin can take minutes to complete a transaction or even hours in the case of payments, due to the chain of validations required to guarantee security.

Ripple digital currencies will total 100 billion. All have already been generated and some will be distributed later. Bitcoins, on the other hand, have a fixed limit of 21 million units, will be created gradually until 2140, and in order to obtain them, when they are released in blocks, it is necessary to have powerful server networks that allow mining operations. Then later they can be traded on spaces like Mt. Gox or Bitcoin-Central.

Finally, the development of cryptocurrencies is closely linked to the spread of digital payment systems as an alternative to traditional cash, giving rise to the phenomenon of social finance. This term refers not only to the possibility of finding financing without resorting to traditional credit channels (along the lines of peer-to-peer credit or crowdfunding) but also to the exploitation of social investment for speculative purposes.

From this point of view, in recent years, algorithm technology has developed exponentially, particularly in two directions: on the one hand, the strand of financial innovations that intervene directly in the management of financial portfolios for mere profit (capital algorithms[33]), and on the other, the use of 'parasitic' algorithms capable of obtaining surplus-value to be reinvested in solidarity and social activities.

In this last field, the most interesting case is certainly the Robin Hood Asset Management Cooperative,[34] founded by a group of activists in Finland and now also established in the home of digital currencies, the Californian Silicon Valley, which is able to finance social projects such as the Cooperativa Integral Catalana and the Faircoop, through the creation of a new peer-to-peer cryptocurrency called Faircoin.[35]

33. Cf. M. Pasquinelli, 'Italian Operaismo and the Information Machine', *Theory, Culture & Society* 32, no. 3 (2015): 49–68.

34. Cf. https://www.robinhoodcoop.org/.

35. Cf. https://www.coinbase.com/it/price/faircoin.

The latter is particularly interesting because, unlike the Bitcoin case, through the creation of blockchain,[36] it seeks to build a financial circuit that cannot be subject to speculative subsumption.

Preliminary conclusions

The monetary and financial sphere, if it was not even considered by the hippy counterculture of the 1960s, was, on the other hand, the one most involved by the cyberculture of the 1980s and 1990s. Indeed, it was in these decades that, thanks to the development of open-source digital technologies, the conditions were created to counter the process of concentration of financial markets and the resulting instability that would reach its peak in the first decade of the new millennium.

This is precisely why the financial counterculture is shot through with strong tensions and travels highly differentiated paths, ending up as the clearest example of the ambiguity of alternative movements overseas. Although it is the theme that most distances itself from the philosophy of the Grateful Dead (and it cannot be otherwise, given that the Dead are the product of the hippy counterculture) it is the one that best describes the essence of Grateful Dead economics.

We will elaborate on this in more detail in the concluding summary chapter. For now, we simply analyse why precisely the issue of finance lends itself to the greatest ambiguity and how the different approaches, while converging in identifying an alternative instrumentation, manifest the widest spectrum of theoretical and political divergence.

In this regard, on the specific issue, it is necessary to distinguish between anarcho-capitalist and anarcho-libertarian approaches.

The former has as its theoretical reference the economist Friedrich von Hayek[37]. In 1976 (at the age of seventy-seven), Hayek felt it urgent

36. Cf. https://www.blockchain.com/.

37. In 2016 at the occupied theatre 'Macao' in Milan, I had the opportunity to chat (for an interview to be published on a movement blog: Effimera.org) with a hacker of Indian origin, but born and living in London, who was part of the small group of those who generated and controlled the blockchain that was the basis for the production of Bitcoins. When I told him, at his request, what I did for a living (professor of Political Economy), he exclaimed, 'Ah, so if you are interested in Bitcoin, you are a follower of Hayek!' I shall let you imagine his amazement when I replied by stating that actually my main theoretical reference was Marx, especially the Marx of the Grundrisse. 'But then you are a

to take a stand against the project of a single European currency. For this reason, he interrupted the writing of the third tome of *Law Legislation and Liberty* to write a new book entitled *Denationalisation of Money: The Argument Refined*,[38] where he proposed, as an alternative to the construction of the Euro, free competition between currencies.

Hayek starts from the Austrian theses on the allocative efficiency of free market exchange, provided that prices are such that they can be considered 'signals' of the kind of information asymmetry that ineluctably arises under conditions of uncertainty. This implies that prices must represent real economic relations, in a context of money neutrality. This is the case if individuals enjoy maximum freedom of decision and choice, thereby promoting the persistence of supply and demand equilibrium and thus price stability. Consequently, inflation is an absolute evil because it prevents proper economic calculation and causes distortions and bad investments, which, if prolonged, can only cause an economic crisis; inflation is the result of excessive money creation, and governments are responsible. The proposal to 'denationalize money', that is, to liberalize its issuance by allowing more parties to print money, is based on three assumptions:

a. anyone who can produce money has an interest in producing as much of it as possible;
b. currency is a good like any other good;
c. for all other goods, it is competition that modulates production to needs.

Hayek concludes that monetary stability would be better assured by a regime of free competition among currencies than by current state management.

Hayek considered his proposal utopian from a political point of view, although from an economic point of view much more easily achievable than the creation of a single European currency. The utopianism lay in the impossibility, in Hayek's eyes, of being able to dismantle the

---

communist!' he exclaimed almost in horror. He began to look at me suspiciously, and the interview never happened again.

38. Cf. F. von Hayek, *The Denationalization of Money. The Argument Refined*, new revised edn (London: The Institute of Economic Analysis, 1978 [orig. edn 1976]). Available online: https://mises.org/library/denationalisat ion-money-argument-refined.

monopoly of state issuance of money, much the same as the hippy counterculture thought, of course in an entirely different context.

Today, thirty years later, Hayek's utopia can be said to have come true. In their book,[39] Bernard Lietaer[40] and Jacqui Dunne[41] document and describe the emergence of private currency competition.

Lietaer and Dunne account for more than 4,000 unofficial, private currencies already operating in today's world. They call them complementary or cooperative, rather than competitive, currencies because they are not competing to replace official currency, but to intervene where available resources are left unused.

Rather, it is in the more specific realm of cryptocurrencies that some element of competition can be observed (between Bitcoin, Leitcoin and Ripple, for example) while competition as far as local currencies are concerned is effectively non-existent, except for that with traditional currency. But, as the name itself implies, local currencies (along the lines of LETS, Sardex, Wir, Bristol Pound) are more about complementary currencies than substitutes for the official one. And it is precisely on this ridge that the slippery slope between the anarcho-capitalist and anarcho-liberal approaches unfolds.

The former makes explicit reference to Hayek's philosophy, denying the role of money as an instrument for representing the social and power relations inherent in the capitalist mode of production.

Paraphrasing Hayek, money is a commodity like all others, and like all others, the money market defines an equilibrium on the basis of the law of supply and demand:[42] an equilibrium defined ex-post, on the basis

39. B. Lietaer and J. Dunne, *Rethinking Money: How New Currencies Turn Scarcity into Prosperity*, (San Francisco: Berret-Koeler Publisher, 2013). For reference, see P. Ferrara, 'Rethinking Money: The Rise of Hayek's Private Competing Currencies', May 2013. Available online: http://www.forbes.com/sites/peterferrara/2013/03/01/rethinking-money-the-rise-of-hayeks-private.competing-currencies/.

40. B. Lietaer, who has a PhD in Economics from MIT, worked as an official at the Central Bank of Belgium and was chairman of Belgium's electronic payment system. He has been an architect of the EU: *Business Week* named him 'world's top currency trader' in 1992.

41. J. Dunne is a journalist (award-winning) and a leader in promoting the development of environmentally friendly technologies.

42. The Law of Supply and Demand states that the equilibrium price of a market is determined by the intersection of market supply and market demand, defined as the summation of individual supply and demand, with

of the desires of individuals who move freely regardless of their social status or occupational status in such a way that no economic agent is able to influence the same equilibrium. Individuals, therefore, far from being subjected to social hierarchies, all have equal opportunities and freedom to make decisions – the only differences between them are subjective preferences.

Whether we are talking about currencies or financial securities, the reasoning does not change, and a superficial analysis – such as that propagated by the economic and journalistic mainstream – seems to support the hypothesis that we are moving in a competitive market where operators are price-takers and there is total freedom of access. Is it not true that the volatility of exchange rates and stock market indices is an indication of very high price flexibility? And is it not true that where there is high price flexibility we are in the presence of markets where the law of supply and demand is sovereign, with no possibility of interference by individual human behaviour?

We have already discussed how such a vision is pure illusion and that the *mimetic rationality*[43] that moves financial markets creates, on the one hand, a growing hierarchy of power and conditioning such that a few financial operators (the large securities dealers companies, SIMs)

no individuals able to influence that price. They are referred to as *price-taker*, thus defining highly competitive markets. More specifically, this law states that when imprinted with an excess of demand over supply, price tends to rise and vice versa.

43. Mimetic rationality refers to that logic of behaviour whereby an individual, in the presence of high uncertainty, imitates the behaviours of those whom he or she believes to be better informed and more authoritative because, rightly or wrongly, they have endowed themselves with high reputations. Such behaviour results in few traders (those who manage high financial portfolios) being able to define the dominant financial conventions from a speculative perspective. It should also be borne in mind that self-fulfilling expectations operate in financial markets: for example, if we all convince ourselves that a certain security will increase in value (because it is purchased in massive doses by a large financed operator – for example, Goldman Sachs), the increase in demand for that security, involving excess demand, will actually lead to an increase in that value. This process, today, is accentuated precisely by the use of algorithms that automatically set such processes in motion. Cf. A. Orléan, *De l'euphorie à la panique: penser la crise financière* (Cepremap, Eitions Rue d'Ulm, 2009).

define the dominant financial conventions and, on the other hand, at the same time, a mass of small, passive and subordinate operators. So much for equal exchange opportunities!

The result is that such complementary currencies are far from also being alternative currencies. In fact, if all currencies that are unofficial, that is, not issued by a supranational operator (such as a public institution) can be said to be complementary, they are not necessarily also alternative.

In this second strand, on the other hand, lies the more strictly anarcho-libertarian thought. In recent years, precisely to avoid processes that capture and subsume these currencies within the financial hierarchies, thereby depowering anti-systemic alternatives, a strand of thought has emerged. This perspective seeks to fuse elements of autonomous Marxist theory (neo-workerist thought) with hacker knowledge to construct an alternative currency. Such a currency could underpin a different financial circuit and enable the reappropriation of the commons, which today, expropriated, serves as the lever on which the profits and rents (in short, inequality) of contemporary bio-cognitive capitalism are built. We call this alternative (and not just complementary) money of the commonwealth or commoncoin.[44]

We believe that it is along these lines that research will need to be set in the future. We are, thus, in agreement with Marco Sachy aka Radium when he writes:

> The literature on the Commonwealth (Negri and Hardt) and Common Goods (Ostrom) – and even earlier that on Italian post-workerism (Lotringer and Marazzi) – offer a desirable ideological basis and invite the translation of the values of re-appropriation of bio-power by the multitude as a function of avoiding disadvantageous systemic configurations such as the hierarchies and compartmentalization imposed by the mechanisms of official/conventional money creation and circulation. The emancipatory values put forward in the post-modern, bio-political and antagonistic literature show how the declination of a monetary system as a common good and its expression in a social and self-managed version of the crypto-blockchain are, today, the elements that inform the re-appropriation of the power of money creation and circulation by civil society's in a decentralized, distributed and dis-intermediate (exodus) manner

44. For a survey, see Braga and Fumagalli (eds), *La moneta del comune*.

with respect to the banking system. The provocation lies in testing whether with crypto-blockchain we can return to an out. Specifically, through the empathic design of distributed payment systems, it is possible to develop software that changes the social behavior of the user in a pro-active sense from the user's own perspective.[45]

45. M. Sachy aka Radium, 'Freecoin: la cripto-blockchain come bene comune', in Braga and Fumagalli (eds), *La moneta del comune*, 145.

Chapter 6

DESIRING SUBJECTIVITIES AND CALIFORNIAN IDEOLOGY: TOWARDS A NEW FORM OF SUBSUMPTION?

Living labour and dead labour

There is a substantial difference between the hippy counterculture of the 1960s and the cyber counterculture of the 1990s.

In the 1960s, the relationship between the human being (with his body, his nerves, his muscles, his brain, his heart, his eros) and the machine was a relationship between separate realms: on the one hand, the human being, living work; on the other hand, the machine, dead work. The relationship between life and death was clear and materially tractable. From the inner human perspective, the machine was something external and tangible, *separate from itself*.

From the 1990s to the present, that separation is no longer so clear. The machine becomes machinic and loses some of its materiality: the gears of the Taylorist machine become increasingly linguistic and relational. Matter defines the casing, the box, but its functioning depends less and less on a mechanistic-rigid automation process and more and more on the cognitive-relational faculties of the human being. Using language as the main tool of machinic functioning changes the nexus of dependence between human beings and machines typical of Tayloristic technologies. In digital technologies, the despotism of the machine is diminished.

But what direction does such a hybrid of human and machine take? Is it the machine that becomes humanized or is it rather the human being that becomes machinized? Do we witness the human becoming of the machine or rather the machinic becoming of man?

It is not possible to give an answer, and it is precisely on such ambiguity that the process of liberating the human being from the 'industrial-military' apparatus that had defined the enemy to be overthrown by the anti-authoritarian and libertarian movements of the 1960s unravels and is consumed.

The cyber counterculture, starting in the early 1970s with the first digital experiments, has always operated with the aim of 'humanizing' the machine, controlling and directing it according to human needs, in a contrast of free and open participation, outside any hierarchy of power.

The slogan 'computer to the people' expressed this will, and the struggle for open-source against intellectual property rights and the free circulation of knowledge and information was its social-political corollary. The libertarian spirit was thus passed down from the hippy counterculture to today's cyberculture.

However, fifty years after the first experiments in the socialization of information technology and thirty years after Barlow's declaration of the independence of cyberspace, we can now say that this dream has hardly come true, although it has opened breaches in the way of acting and thinking that should not be overlooked at all.

To answer this question, it is necessary to resolve a problematic knot that is preparatory to it.

The information technology revolution – now also referred to as the third industrial revolution[1] – emerged simultaneously with the rupture marked by the counterculture of the 1960s and the movements critiquing the Fordist paradigm at the same time as the spread of cyberculture. The question we ask is this: what is the cause-effect nexus? Put another way, is the cyberculture that emerged in the mid-1990s the origin and influence of the information technology revolution or is it the consequence of it?

Olivier Fraissé's essay[2] analyses how the hippy counterculture was a rebellion against Fordism and how that rebellion began to prefigure a

---

1. Cf. J. Rifkin, *The Third Industrial Revolution: How Lateral Power Is Transforming Energy, the Economy, and the World* (New York: St Martin's Publishing Group, 2011). The first industrial revolution took place in England at the end of the eighteenth century, and the second was the Fordist-Taylorist system that began at the turn of the nineteenth and twentieth centuries. The third was represented by the advent of ICT technologies. Today, there is talk of a possible fourth industrial revolution in the future, following the digital one: the revolution of bio-robotics.

2. Cf. O. Frayssé, 'How the Counterculture Redefined Work for the Age of Internet', in O. Fraissé and M. O'Neil (eds), *Digital Labour and Prosumer Capitalism: The U.S. Matrix* (London: Palgrave Macmillan, 2015), 30–50.

new model of work organization for the digital age. Fraissé speaks of a new organization of labour and not of new models of production, as if to emphasize that the transition from Fordism to bio-cognitive capitalism was nonetheless all internal to capitalist logic and not the outcome of a dialectical synthesis between conservative instances of disciplinary type and liberatory instances capable of going beyond capitalist valorization.

Fred Turner,[3] on the other hand, argues that the hippy counterculture was the incubator of a new economic model that would seek to develop into the digital utopia induced by the possible and alternative friendly use of the new technological machines, founded on language, communication and social cooperation.

These two contributions are not antagonistic to each other, rather complementary. Technological and productive modes, in a capitalist reality, have always been the preconditions for defining the organization of labour, both from the point of view of its legal types and, above all, from the point of view of the qualitative content of labour performance.

It follows that we have nevertheless always remained within a capitalist logic of valorization, a logic that continues to be supported by the two pillars that underlie a capitalist system of production: private property and the exploitation of man over man.

These two typical aspects of capitalism can also be seen in the evolution of the relationship between living labour (the human being) and dead labour (machines). Fordist capitalist valorization (i.e. the extraction of surplus value) was based on the primacy of dead labour over living labour, although it could not do without living labour. In the Fordist paradigm, capital, in fact, cannot do without labour, while labour could do without capital, as the Italian *operaismo* of the 1960s taught us.[4] And this is the assumption (conjugated in a context a thousand miles away) that the American hippy counterculture of the 1960s unwittingly tried to make its own and practice.

In the years of Fordist development, first, of cognitive capitalism and then of bio-cognitive capitalism, however, the relationship shifts: the dead labour of (increasingly linguistic) machines begins to live while

3. Cf. F. Turner, *From Counterculture to Cyberculture. Stewart Brand, The Whole Earth Network and the Rise of Digital Utopianism* (Chicago: The University of Chicago Press, 2006).

4. Cf. M. Tronti, *Workers and Capital* (London: Verso, 2019 [first edition in Italy, 1966]).

the living labour of human beings tends partially to standardize, within, however, a primacy of living labour over dead labour.

And here the matter gets complicated, and the Grateful Dead economy is nothing but the exemplification and implementation of this contradiction. Put another way, using Marxian categories, it could be said that the relationship between concrete and abstract labour is being redefined.

Abstract labour and concrete labour

According to Marx, concrete labour, qualitatively defined, is aimed at producing use-value; abstract labour, on the other hand, is pure extrinsic human labour-power, which is independent of the qualitative aspects and specific determinations referring to the utility of individual jobs and whose quantity determines the value created. In the capitalist system of production, abstract labour is the socially necessary labour to produce a commodity that is realized in the final market, that is, exchange value, on the basis of available technology.

In Fordist industrial capitalism, it was the social man-machine relationship that determined the immanent form of abstract labour, which was translated into exchange value of material commodities. In bio-cognitive capitalism, we see, on the other hand, the development of the hegemony of cognitive-relational labor, namely:

> labor that creates intangible products: knowledge, information, communication, linguistic or emotional relations.[5]

This shift implies two ruptures with the previous paradigm.

First, there is the redefinition of the work day in which the division between work time and leisure time blurs. In industrial capitalism, workers produced almost exclusively during the hours they spent in the factory. This depended on the need to combine mechanical means of production with labour-power, and this could take place only in precise and adequate places, thus defining the form of abstract labour and placing a clear separation from concrete, reproductive labour.

5. Cf. A. Negri, *Movimenti nell'Impero. Passaggi e paesaggi* (Milan: Raffaelo Cortina Editore, 2006), 159.

Second, the dematerialization of fixed capital brings into vogue a new, all-too-'human' relationship between means of production and labour-power. Indeed, in immaterial production, the body of labour-power, in addition to containing the faculty of labour, also serves as a container for the functions typical of fixed capital, of the means of production as a sedimentation of codified knowledge, historically acquired knowledge, experience and so on; in short, past, 'experiential' labour.

It follows that the separation between abstract and concrete labour is no longer as clear-cut as in industrial-Fordist capitalism. First, today what Marx called concrete labour, labour that produces use-values, can be renamed creative labour. Indeed, such a term allows for a better grasp of the cerebral input inherent in such activity, whereas the term 'concrete labour', while conceptually synonymous, refers more to the idea of 'doing' than 'thinking', with a reference more to craft work per se.

Rather, within cognitive work activity, one can move indifferently from abstract to creative-concrete work, with outcomes of both exchange-value enhancement and use-value production.

John Halloway writes:

> Here ... lies the center of the class struggle: it is the struggle between creative making and abstract labor. In the past it has been customary to think of the class struggle as the struggle between capital and labor, understanding labor as wage labor, abstract labor, and the working class has often been defined as the class of wage workers. But this is wrong. Wage labor and capital complement each other mutually, the former being a moment of the latter. There is undoubtedly a conflict between wage labor and capital, but it is a relatively superficial conflict. It is a conflict over wage levels, the length of the workday, working conditions – all of these are important but presuppose the existence of capital. The real threat to capital comes not from abstract labor but from useful labor or creative making, since it is creative making that radically opposes capital, that is, its own abstraction. It is creative making that says 'no, we will not let capital rule, we must do what we consider necessary or desirable.[6]

And it is precisely to prevent 'creative making' from taking over abstract labour that in bio-cognitive capitalism the control of the

6. Cf. J. Halloway, 'We Are the Crisis of Abstract Labour', UniNomade workshop, Bologna, 11–12 March 2006.

process of training and learning becomes central, just as the control of the sources of knowledge, through intellectual property rights, is central. Indeed, the processes of formation and learning are inherently ambivalent: to what extent is it possible to distinguish the process of learning aimed at developing one's own culture according to an autonomously chosen logic of liberation and self-determination and the process of formation made necessary to perform labour activity for the purposes of capitalist accumulation? To what extent is it possible today to distinguish within a work day the time socially necessary to produce exchange value from that used to produce use values?

Obviously, it is not possible to provide an adequate answer. Unless one assumes a trending process of *life subsumption*[7] of individuals leading to the total disappearance of use-value and the absolute dominance of exchange value. This would be a chilling prospect of the commodification of all life that would presuppose the reduction of human beings to brain slavery.

Nonetheless, the difficulty of separating concrete and abstract labour is evidenced by the growing importance of the labour-force formation process and the existence of ever-expanding cooperative networks (general intellect) that are always understood as both entrepreneurial and personal investment, as well as, in the last decade, the pervasive spread of social media. This is primarily because, in bio-cognitive capitalism, work, training and relationship form a whole throughout the entire period of active life. It is not just a one-time investment, coinciding with the years of schooling, but a recurring investment over the years of active life that must therefore provide for amortization, just as when one invests in a machine to start a production process anticipating that, at the end of its recurring use, it will have to be replaced with a new machine.

The living reproductive labour of labour-power, its being self-promotional to the point of being available to free activities as long as they are socially recognized and validated, makes it possible to reduce the cost of labour-power to capital and, therefore, to increase surplus value. It could be argued that the amount of reproductive living labour is what allows fixed capital to depreciate because, by reproducing the use-value of labour-power, it reproduces at the same time its capacity to consume capital.

---

7. To the concept of life subsumption we will return shortly.

In bio-cognitive capitalism, alienation is all internal to the individual, it is cerebral alienation, between heart and hand, between the right and left hemispheres of the brain, no longer between internal and external, between participation in production and the outcome of production itself.

From Fordist capitalism to bio-cognitive capitalism

The Fordist valorization process entered a crisis due to the same factors that had caused its success: the standardization of production with the consequent rigid and disciplined organization of labour (based on the figure of the mass worker). In the 1920s and 1930s and then in the post-Second World War period, the rigid automation of production had made it possible to take full advantage of the economies of scale resulting from increased productivity: a productivity that, it should be remembered, depended essentially on the expropriation of worker knowledge for the benefit of machines with the consequent reduction of the human being to a subordinate and alienated appendage of the same machines.

Over the past thirty years, the new process of capitalist accumulation and valorization has been referred to in various ways: the most common, post-Fordism, is also the oldest. However, the term, like all terms that are defined by negation, is not free from ambiguity and different interpretations. The term post-Fordism is intended to refer to that period, which we can date between the crisis of 1975 and the crisis of the early 1990s, in which the process of accumulation and valorization is no longer characterized by the centrality of Fordist material production in the large factory. But at the same time, an alternative paradigm is not yet visible. In the suffix 'post', not surprisingly, what is no longer there is expressed, but what is in the process of becoming is not emphasized. In fact, the post-Fordist phase is characterized by the simultaneous coexistence of several production models: from the Japanese Toyotist model of 'just in time' of Taylorist derivation,[8] to the model of small business industrial

---

8. See, among others, T. Ohno, *Toyota Production System: Beyond Large-scale Production* (New York: Productivity Press Inc., 1995); G. Bonazzi, *Il tubo di cristallo. Modello giapponese e fabbrica integrata alla Fiat* (Bologna: Il Mulino, 1993); M. Revelli, 'Economia e modello sociale nel passaggio tra fordismo e toyotismo', in P. Ingrao and R. Rossanda (eds) *Appuntamenti di fine secolo*

districts,[9] to the development of production chains that tend to internationalize on a hierarchical basis.[10] It is not yet possible to identify a hegemonic paradigm. It is at this stage that the original plinth of the digital revolution begins to develop and it is after the first Gulf War that innovations in the field of transportation and in the field of language and communication (ICT) begin to coagulate around a single, new paradigm of accumulation and valorization. The new capitalist configuration tends to identify the commodity 'knowledge' and 'space' (geographic and virtual) as the new cornerstones on which to base a dynamic capacity for accumulation. Two new dynamic economies of scale are thus being determined that underlie productivity growth (and thus a source of surplus value): learning economies (learning) and network economies (network). The former are related to the process of generation and creation of new knowledge (based on new communication and information technologies), the latter are derived from both district organizational modes (territorial networks or area-systems) and new technologies of knowledge and communication dissemination (and control).

We can name such an accumulation paradigm by the term *cognitive capitalism*:[11]

(Rome: Manifestolibri, 1995), 161–224; B. Coriat, *Penser à l'invers* (Paris: C. Bourgois, 1991).

9. Cfr. M. Priore and C. Sabel, *The Second Industrial Divide. Possibilities for Prosperity* (New York: Productivity Basic Books, 1984); S. Brusco, *Piccole imprese e distretti industriali* (Turin: Rosenberg & Seller, 1989); G. Becattini, *Distretti industriali e sviluppo locale* (Turin: Bollati Boringhieri, 2000). For a critical analysis, cf. M. Lazzarato, Y. Moulier Boutang, A. Negri and G. Santilli, *Des entreprises pas comme le outres* (Paris: Publisud, 1993); A. Fumagalli, 'Lavoro e piccola impresa nell'accumulazione flessibile in Italia. Parte I e Parte II', in *Altreragioni* (1996–7), 5, 6.

10. Cfr. C. Palloix, *L'economia mondiale e le multinazionali*, 2 vols (Milan: Jaca Book, 1979 and 1982); G. Bertin, *Multinationales et propriété industrielle: le contrôle de la tecnologie mondiale* (Parigi: Presse Universitaire du France, 1985).

11. This term was born in France in the early 2000s as part of the research activity of Laboratoire Isys-Matisse, Maison des Sciences Economique, University of Paris I, La Sorbonne, under the direction of Bernard Paulré, and is propagated by the journal *Multitudes* with very diverse writings by A. Corsani, M. Lazzarato, Y. Moulier-Boutang, T. Negri, E. Rullani, C. Vercellone and others. See B. Paulré, 'De la *New Economy* au capitalisme cognitif', *Multitudes* 2 (2000): 25–42; C. Azais, A. Corsani and P. Dieuaide (eds), *Vers un capitalisme cognitif* (Paris: L'Harmattan, 2001); Y. Moulier Boutang, *Cognitive Capitalism*

theterm capitalism designates the permanence, in the metamorphosis, of the fundamental variables of the capitalist system: in particular, the guiding role of profit and the wage ratio or more precisely the different forms of wage labor from which surplus value is extracted; the cognitive attribute highlights the new nature of labor, the sources of valorization and the structure of ownership, on which the process of accumulation is based and the contradictions that this mutation generates.[12]

The centrality of learning and network economies, typical of bio-cognitive capitalism, is being challenged with the beginning of the new millennium following the bursting of the 'Net-Economy' speculative bubble in March 2000. The new cognitive paradigm alone cannot secure the socio-economic system from its structural instability. New liquidity needs to be injected into the financial markets. The ability of financial markets to generate 'value', in fact, is linked to the development of 'conventions' (speculative bubbles) capable of creating tendentially homogeneous expectations that drive major financial players to bet on certain types of financial assets.[13] In the 1990s it was, precisely, the Net

(Hoboken, NJ: John Wiley & Sons, 2012); C. Vercellone (ed.), *Sommes-nous sortis du capitalisme industriel?* (Paris: La Dispute, 2003); A. Corsani, P. Dieuaide, M. Lazzarato, J. M. Monnier, Y. Moulier Boutang, B.Paulré and C. Vercellone, *Le Capitalism cognitif comme sortie de la crise du capitalism industriel. Un programme de recherche* (Paris: Laboratoire ISYS-Matisse du Centre d'économie de la Sorbonne de l'Université de Paris 1, 2004). For more up-to-date research, see C. Vercellone (ed.), *Capitalismo Cognitivo* (Rome: Manifestolibri, 2006);); A. Fumagalli, *Bioeconomia e capitalismo cognitivo. Verso un nuovo paradigma di accumulazione* (Rome: Carocci, 2007). See also the monographic issue 'Le capitalisme cognitif. Apports et perspectives', *European Journal of Economic and Social Systems* 20, no. 1 (2007), edited by A. Fumagalli and C. Vercellone, with contributions, in addition to those of the editors, by A. Arvidsson, L. Cassi, A. Corsani, P. Dieuaide, S. Lucarelli, J. M. Monnier and B. Paulré.

12. Cf. D. Lebert and C. Vercellone, 'Il ruolo della conoscenza nella dinamica di lungo periodo del capitalismo: l'ipotesi del capitalismo cognitivo', in C. Vercellone (ed.), *Capitalismo cognitivo* (Rome: Manifestolibri, 2006), 22. On English, see A. Fumagalli, A. Giuliani, S. Lucarelli and C. Vercellone, *Cognitive Capitalism, Welfare and Labour: The Commonfare Hypothesis* (London: Routledge, 2019).

13. Cf. A. Orléan, *De l'euphorie à la panique: penser la crise financière* (Paris: Rue d'Ulm, 2009).

Economy; in the 2000s the attraction came from the development of Asian markets (with China joining the WTO in December 2001) and real estate. Today it tends to focus on the resilience of European welfare. Regardless of the dominant type of convention, contemporary capitalism is perpetually looking for new social and vital realms to engulf and commodify, to the point of increasingly affecting what are the vital faculties of human beings. This is why in recent years people have begun to talk about bio-economy and bio-cognitive capitalism.[14]

At this point, it should be clear to the reader how the term we use in these pages is nothing more than the mix of cognitive capitalism and bio-capitalism: bio-cognitive capitalism as the terminological definition of contemporary capitalism.

This metamorphosis of the capitalist valorization process has also been accompanied, conveyed and fomented by the rise of new subjectivities and desiring surpluses along the ambiguous ridge between consensual and appreciative participation and transgressive and confrontational rupture.

The 'California ideology' and the myth of social innovation

In this context, a critical reading of the relationship between technology, culture and innovation (including social innovation) is inescapable.

'A strange alliance of writers, hackers, capitalists and artists on America's West Coast gave birth to a heterogeneous orthodoxy of the information age: the California ideology.' Thus wrote, more than thirty years ago, in 1995, Richard Barbrook and Andy Cameron in a famous essay entitled 'The California Ideology'[15]. They continued:

> This new faith has emerged from a bizarre fusion of the cultural bohemianism of San Francisco with the hi-tech industries of Silicon Valley. Promoted in magazines, books, TV programs,

14. Cf. A. Fumagalli, 'Bio-Cognitive Capitalism', in B. Skeggs, S. R. Farris, A. Toscano and S. Bromberg (eds), *The SAGE Handbook of Marxism*, vol. 3 (2022), ch. 84, 1537–55.

15. Cf. R. Barbrook and A. Cameron, 'The Californian Ideology', in *Science as Culture* 6, no. 1 (1996): 44–72 [a first version was published in *Mute Magazine*, 1995]. Available online: http://www.imaginaryfutures. net/2007/04/17/the-californian-ideology-2.

websites, newsgroups and Net conferences, the Californian Ideology promiscuously combines the free-wheeling spirit of the hippies and the entrepreneurial zeal of the yuppies. This amalgamation of opposites has been achieved through a profound faith in the emancipatory potential of new information technologies. In the digital utopia, everybody will be both hip and rich. Not surprisingly, this optimistic vision of the future has been enthusiastically embraced by computer nerds, slacker students, innovative capitalists, social activists, trendy academics, futurist bureaucrats and opportunistic politicians across the USA.[16]

Despite its great influence in the international debate, and especially in the US, the concept of 'California ideology' in Italy has remained unknown, even to much of the public interested in these issues.

With that term, we want to refer here to the emergence of a new composition of living labour at the time of the birth of digital technologies: in a context where, as we already mentioned, the relationship between human being and machine increasingly interpenetrate into a hybrid with a difficult definition.

Richard Barbrook and Andy Cameron speak of the emergence of the virtual class: a class that is transversal to the traditional dichotomy between subordinate (worker) and corporate (entrepreneur) labour, that goes beyond class struggle to constitute a kind of labour aristocracy. It is the

> techno-intelligence of cognitivist scientists, engineers, computer experts, video game developers, and all communication specialists .... Unable to subject them to assembly-line discipline or replace them with machines, managers employed these intellectual workers through fixed-term contracts.[17]

This is the birth of cognitive-relational work, on the one hand, and creative (or supposedly so) work, on the other. From this point of view, the assonance with another famous text that, a few years later, will coin the term creative class is not surprising. We refer to the well-known

16. http://www.imaginaryfutures.net/2007/04/17/the-californian-ideol ogy-2, 1.

17. http://www.imaginaryfutures.net/2007/04/17/the-californian-ideol ogy-2.

text by Richard Florida,[18] in which the emphasis is placed on the advent of a new social class, the creative class, capable of transforming the ways in which we communicate, work and create community in the twenty-first century. This new class, consisting at the same time of scientists and humanists, literati and technologists, artists and novelists would be configured as a new social group capable of harmonizing the philosophy of the bohemian and that of the bourgeois, according to the terminology of the 'Bobo' coined by David Brooks in *Bobos in Paradise*.[19] The economic function of such a class would then be to generate new ideas, new technologies and/or creative content, revolutionizing the old hierarchical and formal ways of managing the economy and labour. If this new culture represents a mixture of bourgeois and bohemian values, the underlying principles should be traced back to characteristics such as creativity, individualism, difference and merit, since

> for members of the Creative Class, every aspect and every manifestation of technological, cultural and economic creativity is interconnected and inseparable from the others.[20]

From these analyses it would seem that a new composition of labour has arisen. Now there is no doubt that the structural transformations developed in technological and productive organizations by the advent of bio-cognitive capitalism have profoundly affected subjectivities and modes of work performance both at the organizational and – I would say – anthropological levels.

The new native-digital generations are on a completely different wavelength and linguistic-communicative channels are incomparable with the generation of the hippy counterculture, which was inevitably immersed by Fordist disciplinary authoritarianism and against which it had rebelled.

But one can only talk about labour composition effectively if one analyses the evolution of the ownership structure and the capital-labour

18. Cf. R. Florida, *The Rise of the Creative Class: And How It's Transforming Work, Leisure, Community and Everyday Life* (New York: Basic Books, 2002).

19. Cf. D. Brooks, *Bobos in Paradise: The New Upper Class and How They Got There* (New York: Simon & Schuster, 2004), where *Bobos* is derived from the mix of bourgeois and bohemian.

20. Cfr. L. Fuiano, 'L'emergere della "nuova" classe creativa', 2006. Available online: http://www.Politica online.it/?p=368 (my translation).

relationship. By not delving into these issues, the Californian ideology is nothing more than a recognition of that capacity for social innovation that has always characterized the recovery of capital. No more nor less than is happening in these years, in the aftermath of the greatest period of crisis capitalism can remember, equal if not greater than the great recession of the 1930s.

Even today, in fact, there is much talk of social innovation: a social innovation that, thanks to the evolution of communication and digital technologies and the spread of social media, is capable of organizing and 'capturing' what today has become the basis of capitalist accumulation: social cooperation, the outcome of the power of that general intellect that cyberculture itself has allowed to emerge. If ten years ago, at the dawn of the spread of flexibility and the precarization of labour, there was much talk of creativity, networks (short or long), cumulativity, immateriality, in a word, network economy, today the modes and spaces of bio-economic accumulation are named: co-working, co-housing, recognition, merit, cooperation, complementary currencies, in a word, sharing economy.

*From the network economy to the sharing
economy: ownership, control and sharing*

In the Western context, the debate on the idea of property has always focused on the dichotomy between private/individual and public/state ownership.

It is well known that in the US the issue of private property has an almost 'constitutive' as well as 'constituent' significance, starting from the Far-West myth and up to the point that private property coincides with individual freedom and individual freedom coincides with consumer sovereignty.

'I defend the family; therefore, I support the free market.' The *cogito, ergo sum* of the US conservative grassroots world is this. It is property rights, as far-reaching and radical as possible, the princely instrument which, by keeping state influence away from family affairs, makes concrete the protection of nascent life, natural morality, free education and so on. Not only the sovereignty of the consumer but also of the taxpayer, the citizen, that is, who buys by paying and who by paying controls. Who demands, in short, to know how his or her money is used, who demands to know what the costs of the services his or her money buys are, questioning price increases to discriminate between legitimate earnings and illegal profits, who demands daily transparency of the administrations, management and politics to which he or she lends his or her money so that the investment pays off.

Conversely, alternative movements, whether the counterculture of the 1960s or the cyberculture of the 1990s, have in common the questioning of the individual property but not of the individual and his freedom. Sharing from this point of view is part of the way alternative movements act.

However, rarely, outside the experiments of the 'communes' as a form of exodus, have such sharing processes given rise to the emergence of alternative production models. The 'enterprise' form has always been the main economic-legal reference. This has meant and still means that the production of exchange-value is prevalent over the production of use-value, that (individual) profit is therefore not questioned, even in the – already mentioned – mixture of concrete and abstract labour.

We have seen how this issue has favoured the emergence of cyberculture. Today we can say that in most cases, the entrepreneurial spirit has prevailed over the social spirit. From this point of view, the entrepreneurial activism of Grateful Dead Inc. is very emblematic. It encapsulates all the characteristics of today's capitalism: cooperation and social innovation, consumer loyalty, and experimentation with new monetary forms. And it cannot be otherwise in a context of immaterial and symbolic production that makes the alternative nature of life and culture its trademark.

We are, thus, in the context of a sharing economy, where the processes of subsumption of labour to capital are modified and take new shape. We will address this aspect as the concluding parable of these notes.

The new modes of subsumption of labour to capital: can Grateful Dead economics be a possible antidote?

In bio-cognitive capitalism, real subsumption and formal subsumption are two sides of the same coin and feed off each other. They jointly give rise to a new form of subsumption, which we can call life or general intellect subsumption.[21] This new form of modern capitalist accumulation highlights certain aspects that underlie the crisis of

---

21. Cf. A. Fumagalli, 'The Concept of Subsumption of Labour to Capital. Towards the Life Subsumption in Bio-cognitive Capitalism', in E. Fisher and C. Fuchs (eds), *Reconsidering Value and Labor in the Digital Age* (London: Palgrave Macmillan, 2015), 224–45.

industrial capitalism. It involves analysing the new sources of wealth (and increasing returns) in bio-cognitive capitalism. These sources derive from the crisis of the model of technical and social division generated by the first industrial revolution and carried to extremes by Taylorism, and are nurtured by the role and diffusion of knowledge that obeys 'a cooperative social rationality that escapes the restrictive conception of human capital'.[22] As a result, immediate work time is challenged as the main and only productive time with the effect that actual and certified work time is no longer the only measure of productivity and the only guarantee of access to income. There is thus a twist in the traditional labour-value theory toward a new theory of value, in which the concept of work is increasingly characterized by 'knowledge' and permeated with life activity. We can call this the transition to a theory of value-knowledge or theory of life-value,[23] if knowledge and life tend to feed off each other and where the main fixed capital is man 'in whose brain resides the knowledge accumulated by society'.[24]

When life becomes labour-power, working time is no longer measurable in standard units (hours, days). The work day no longer has any limits except natural ones. We are in the presence of formal subsumption and absolute plus-value extraction. When life becomes labour-power because the brain becomes machine, that is, 'fixed capital and variable capital at the same time', the intensification of labour performance reaches its maximum: we are thus in the presence of real subsumption and extraction of relative surplus-value.

Such a combination of the two forms of subsumption – what we can call *life subsumption*[25] – needs a new system of social regulation and political governance.

The wage process has historically been the main mode that has enabled capital's command over labour in the presence of formal subsumption. In contrast, the technical composition and division of labour, both as an expression of the separation of man and machine

---

22. Cf. C. Vercellone and R. Herrera in 'Trasformazioni della divisione del lavoro e General Intellect. Una critica marxista delle teorie della crescita endogena', in C. Vercellone (ed.), *Capitalismo cognitivo* (Rome: Manifestolibri, 2006).

23. Cf. C. Morini and A. Fumagalli, 'Life Put to Work: Towards a Life Theory of Value', *Euphemera* 10, no. 3/4 (2010): 234–52. Available online: https://ephe merajournal.org/sites/default/files/2022-01/10-3morinifumagalli.pdf.

24. K. Marx, *Grundrisse* (London: Penguin Books, 1973), 725.

25. Cf. Fumagalli, 'The Concept of Subsumption of Labour to Capital'.

and as the disciplining and hierarchy of labour performance, has characterized the phase of real subsumption.

If the process of both direct and indirect wage-making[26] is still the instrument that, in part, fosters formal subsumption (think of the wage-making of care work, (re)production and learning, although it is still non-existent with regard to other productive labour activities, such as consumption and social relations, as well as leisure and cultural activities), in bio-cognitive capitalism, the technical division of labour and the separation between man and machine are no longer the main factors that fuel real subsumption.

To this must be added what Federico Chicchi, Emanuele Leonardi and Stefano Lucarelli, in a recent publication,[27] call the dissolution of the wage relationship.

> It is in fact the explosion of the wage dynamic as the driving force of value creation that leads us to question the modes of contemporary exploitation and the logics that inform them by problematizing and forcing the heuristic potential of Marxian categories of analysis.

Productivity growth is increasingly dependent on the exploitation of dynamic learning and network economies, that is, increasing returns to scale that are fed by the passage of time that is no longer measurable from outside the work performance, just as factory production time was measured by the stopwatch applied to machine times and rhythms. Learning and networking, the generation and dissemination of knowledge, are intrinsically linked to the subjectivity, competence and individuality of the worker/employee. The times of learning and relationship – the times of the general intellect – become objectively

26. Indirect retribution refers to the remuneration of an employment relationship that is not characterized by elements of prescriptiveness of tasks legally defined and subordinated on the basis of contractual agreements, but rather the remuneration of services that are formally independent and autonomous, although in fact subject to unilateral heterodirection. We refer, for example, to the various collaboration contracts that are increasingly common today and for the most part related to cognitive forms of work (VAT numbers, work for third parties, consultancy of various kinds) of a single-contractor type.

27. Cf. F. Chicchi, E. Leonardi and S. Lucarelli, *Logiche dello sfruttamento. Oltre la dissoluzione del rapporto salariale* (Verona: Ombre Corte, 2016), 15 (my translation).

unmeasurable and therefore not directly controllable and disciplined. In such activities, work performance tends to break out of a relationship of wage subalternity. It takes on the forms of self-entrepreneurship, typical of the sharing economy. In order for this new social organization of labour to be guided by the logic of profit resulting from its process of expropriation and exploitation, it is necessary to redefine new instruments of control. These are no longer based solely on the simple and direct discipline of individuals, but increasingly on forms of indirect social control. Deleuze had already identified this shift, starting with Foucault's analysis:

> Foucault placed disciplinary societies between the 18th and 19th centuries; they reach their apogee in the early 20th. They proceed to the organization of large environments of confinement. The individual does not cease to move from one closed environment to another, each endowed with its own laws: first the family, then the school ("you are no longer in the family"), then the barracks ("you are no longer in school"), then the factory, now and then the hospital, eventually the prison, which is the environment of confinement par excellence.[28]

Deleuze then added, with reference to the crisis of the 1970s:

> We find ourselves in a generalized crisis of all environments of confinement, prison, hospital, factory, school and family. The family is an "interior" in crisis like all other interiors, school, vocational, etc. Relevant ministers never stop announcing reforms deemed necessary. Reform the school, reform industry, reform the hospital, reform the army, reform the prison: but everyone knows that these institutions are finished, with more or less expiration. It is only a matter of managing their agony and keeping people occupied until new forces press at the gates. These are the societies of control that are about to replace the disciplinary societies. "Control" is the name Burroughs proposed to designate this new monster and which Foucault recognizes as our near future.[29]

28. G. Deleuze, 'L'autre journal', no. 1 (May 1990), now in G. Deleuze, *Pourparlers (1972–1990)* (Paris: Minuit, 1990), 240–7. Available online: http://www.ecn.org/filiarmonici/Deleuze.html (my translation).

29. Deleuze, 'L'autre journal'.

Deleuze points out that in societies of control, the individual is defined not by a 'signature' and 'a number' but by 'a digit': the digit is a kind of password, access code, while disciplinary societies are regulated by passwords both from the point of view of integration and resistance. The digital language of control is made up of digits that mark access to information, or rejection.

> One is no longer faced with the mass/individual pair. Individuals have become 'dividuals', and the masses statistical samples, data, markets or 'banks'.[30]

This is the dark side of the digital revolution, the one that the early hacker movements had strenuously fought against and that today seems to be taking over with the spread of meta-data, its concentration and unilateral use, thanks in part to the new communicative devices that after 11 September 2001, place the security emergency as a moment that becomes the norm (and therefore the rule) at the expense of any form of even formally bourgeois decisionism.

The society of control is the governance of life subsumption.

The problematic nodes of today: from the relationship between time and being to the relationship between time and desire

The speed of change and, especially, its acceleration in the last forty years have been very high. We have to recognize that somee of the factors that fostered this acceleration were the counter-cultural and anti-systemic movements of the 1960s and 1990s. The former broke the veneer of immobilist conformity that Fordist social discipline had imposed, the latter pointed from the side of technology and new forms of social organization to an escape route and a direction that even today has not been exhausted.

The topic of accelerationism has been the subject of increasing attention, not only because of the publication of a well-known manifesto[31] but also and especially because it has re-proposed the theme of the future of humanity. The thesis is as follows: the 2008 crisis

30. Deleuze, 'L'autre journal'.

31. N. Srnicek and A. Williams, 'Manifesto for an Accelerationist Politics', in J. Johnson (ed.), *Dark Trajectories: Politics of the Outside* (Miami: Name, 2013).

did not change the fortunes of global capitalism, on the contrary, it strengthened it; the protest movements that emerged in that crisis (the various Occupy and 15M) did not affect it in any way; the 'primitivist' responses (back to the land, local policies, etc.) fielded by the radical left proved to be rearguard; and meanwhile, the ecological, social and economic disasters caused by neo-liberalism have undermined the very idea of the future.

Srnicek and Williams then explain that 'the future needs to be built'.[32] And it will have to be a 'more modern future – an alternative modernity that neoliberalism is inherently incapable of generating'; not only because 'capitalism is an unjust and perverse system', but also because it is 'a system that holds back progress. Our technological development has been suppressed by capitalism as much as it has been unleashed by it.' There is therefore a need for a politics 'at ease with a modernity of abstraction, complexity, globality and technology': an *accelerationist politics*, precisely.

In fact, it is necessary to be more capitalist than capitalists to produce the crisis of capitalism, especially in its neo-liberal version. The contradictions that open up in the new human-machine relationship, in the structural instability of finance, in growing income inequality, if not alleviated and corrected – if that was ever possible – represent the endogenous crisis of the system more than any form of opposition and antagonism.

Assuming that such theses are realistic, there remains an underlying question, which cannot be answered: if capitalism were to collapse by its own contradictions in the absence of any 'saving' antagonistic force, the first to pay the price would be those very people who suffer the pains of capitalism today.

There are two critical aspects in particular: the relationship between time and being, that is, between power and autonomy, and the relationship between time and desire.

The psychedelic music of the Grateful Dead, with its very long improvisational jams, dilates time; the counterculture of the 1970s wants to recapture it for its human-scale use; the electronic music of the 1990s emphasizes its technological acceleration in line with the cyber counterculture's aspirations for digital liberation. The high-tech music

32. Srnicek and Williams, 'Manifesto for an Accelerationist Politics'.

of the last decade confirms this. In this regard, there are those who speak of *accelerationist music!*[33]

We are thus faced with a twisting of the relationship between the passage of time and the definition of one's subjectivity. If the valorization process of bio-cognitive capitalism – as we have written – is increasingly based on knowledge and space, the outcome of the valuing of the vital faculties of individuals, we are witnessing, on the one hand, the emergence of a possible economy of abundance (knowledge and space, if understood as internecine space, being not subject to scarcity), on the other hand, the recognition of the potential of the individual when it connects with social cooperation. The new constraint becomes the time factor (twenty-four hours a day), the only variable that is subject to scarcity today.

On this trade-off are grafted the contradictions of the present. The attempts being experienced today speak to us of the possibility of imagining a world of 'sharing' such as to be able to overcome the conflict, always immanent between individual liberation and the idea of community.

The concept of the commons, beyond the dichotomy between private and public,[34] now represents a prospect for the future. We talk about the commons as a possible future horizon of a new mode of production, aimed at the production of use-value and not exchange-value. That is, the commonwealth as a new way of organizing the productive enhancement that is inherent within us, deciding how, how much, where and for whose benefit we 'produce'.

From this point of view – differently from the issue of the commons – the commonwealth could enable self-management of one's time and ecological sustainability, resolving the dialectic between time and being. At the same time, it is an expression of desire and potential, at the very moment when the production of use-values turns out to be central to the communitarian organization of production. No longer just 'from each according to his abilities, to each according to his needs' but also 'from each according to his potentialities, to each according to his dreams'.

33. Cf. V. Mattioli, 'Appunti per una discografia accelerazionista', 13 April 2015. Available online: http://www.prismomag.com/appunti-per-una-discogra fia-accelerazionista/.

34. Cf. M. Hardt and A. Negri, *Commonwealth* (Harvard: Harvard University Press, 2011).

The hippy communes of the 1960s had tried to realize this perspective. The Grateful Dead's home at 710 Ashbury Street was an example of this. They did not hold up because they had an anti-technological attitude and above all were unable to secure monetary and financial independence. Their chance of survival lay in isolating themselves from the traditional world that they wanted to fight and transform. The exodus, from this point of view, was a 'destitute' exodus. Today, if anything, a 'constituent' exodus would be necessary.

Instead, the cyber counterculture aimed to contaminate the mainstream world, with the goal of exalting the individuality that is present in each of us. But instead of contaminating, we often became contaminated. As Paolo Godani writes about the processes of individual subjectivization:

> The device of individualization, which we have seen to be a decisive site of contemporary technologies of power, is exactly the opposite of this affirmation of power, meaning and event.[35]

The life subsumption process of bio-cognitive capitalism operates through that social and technological innovation that the cyber counterculture hoped would be liberating but which too often turned out to be a cage. The individualist and anti-communitarian obsession of US-based libertarian thought thus proved victorious over the hacker communitarian spirit of the early days. We have already pointed out how the litmus test is represented by the fact that any initiative, even the most alternative and 'revolutionary' possible, finds its explicitness in the capitalist matrix 'enterprise' form. And equally, such 'enterprise' – the second no less important aspect – moves within all the monetary and financial constraints imposed by capitalist command. Clearly, under such conditions, it is inevitable that any alternative activity – unless it remains marginal and thus insignificant – is forced to come to terms with market hierarchies and thus be vitally subsumed. And it is in such a way that capitalism, feeding on the innovations of those who want to transform it, if not to tear it down, can modernize itself and overcome the structural crises it periodically generates.

35. Cf. P. Godani, 'La vita comune. Per una filosofia e una politica oltre l'individuo', *Opera viva*, 4 July 2016. Available online: http://operaviva.info/la-vita-comune/ (my translation).

Brief concluding note: toward a financial psychedelic?

Counter-cultural and underground productions have always represented a strong innovative thrust to counter the structural instability of capitalism, in its different phases. In all fields, from the arts to economics, politics and society, they have fostered the emergence of new progressive and progressive subjectivities. At the same time, they created contradictions and fracture lines that pushed history forward.

   If we had to define in a few words the legacy that the counter-cultural and cyber movements have left us to date, we could say that they anticipated the current forms of capitalist valorization. But the resulting outcome has been quite different from what was hoped for. In fact, the current economic context is characterized by two phenomena that today have redefined the core of accumulation processes, which were not completely foreseeable at the time: globalization and financialization, with the consequent fragmentation of subjectivities and the need to rethink adequate processes of recomposition of a labour that increasingly coincides with and subsumes human existence itself. It should be noted that both the countercultural movements of the 1960s and the cyber movements have always sought to value human life with the goal of creating the preconditions for a liberated and self-determined world. But what has ultimately been lacking is the definition of a toolbox that can guarantee this autonomy. And when we speak of autonomy we refer not only to the ability to develop free and conscious self-determination of the individual culturally and politically but also to the ability to equip oneself with economic and financial sustainability. The latter is in fact the necessary, though not sufficient, condition for counter-cultural and alternative initiatives to be able to sustain themselves and ensure economic sustainability without running the risk of being subsumed. With this in mind, the first elements of this new toolbox consist of:

– the implementation of an alternative currency, capable of defining an alternative monetary-financial circuit, not assimilated to the capitalist one, conditioned by the financial oligarchies but rather aimed at creating the basis for financial psychedelics from below;[36]

36. Cf. E. Braga and A. Fumagalli (eds), *La moneta del comune. La sfida dell'istituzione finanziaria del comune* (Rome: DeriveApprodi – Alfabeta, 2015). In English, 'CommonCoin – a Tool for Alternative Economies, New Social Currencies and Basic Income'. Available online: https://www.spacesandcit

– the introduction of an unconditional basic income, understood as remuneration for life put to value, financed by the same alternative currency.[37]

Then, we can begin to speak about *commonism* within an exodus, this time a constituent one.[38]

ies-toolkit.com/tools/commoncoin-a-tool-for-alternative-economies-new-soc ial-currencies-and-basic-income. See also the website: https://commonfare. net/en.

37. About unconditional basic income, there is a wide literature. See, as example: https://www.ubie.org/who-we-are/.

38. Cf. P. de Bagato, 'Comun(e)ismo. Lettera a Michele quarantun anni dopo', in C. Morini and P. Vignola (eds), *Piccola Enciclopedia Precaria* (Milan: Agenzia X, 2015), 229–32.

LIST OF GRATEFUL DEAD'S LIVE CONCERTS, QUOTED IN THE BOOK

Polo Field in San Francisco's Golden Gate Park on 14 January 1967: https://archive.org/details/gd67-01-14.sbd.vernon.9108.sbeok.shnf

Straight Theater, Haight Street, San Francisco on 23 July 1967: https://archive.org/details/gd1967-07-23.sbd.bershaw-wulf.5418.shnf

Haight Street, San Francisco, on 3 March 1968: https://archive.org/details/gd68-03-03.aud.vernon.9374.sbeok.shnf

Columbia University, New York City, on 3 May 1968: https://archive.org/details/gd1968-05-00.sbd.currier.5427.sbeok.shnf; video: https://www.youtube.com/watch?v=zq8sp6WF3bQ

The Matrix, San Francisco, on 16 December 1968: https://archive.org/details/gd68-12-16.sbd.hartbeats.4529.sbeok.shnf

Kresge Plaza, Massachusetts Institute of Technology, Boston, on 6 May 1970: https://archive.org/details/gd1970-05-06.sbd.gans-hall.95.shnf

Euphoria Ballroom, San Raphael, California on 1 July 1970: https://archive.org/details/gd70-07-16.sbd.clugston.6485.sbeok.shnf

Old Renaissance Faire, in Veneta, Oregon, on 2 August 1972: https://archive.org/details/gd72-08-27.sbd.orf.3328.sbeok.shnf

Dane County Coliseum on 15 February 1973: https://archive.org/details/gd1973-02-15.sbd.hall.1580.shnf

Seattle Center Arena, Seattle, on 26 June 1973: https://archive.org/details/gd73-06-26.sbd.cotsman.12076.sbeok.shnf

Grand Prix Racecourse, Watkins Glen, NY, on 27 July 1973: https://archive.org/details/gd73-07-27.sbd.weiner.180.sbeok.shnf

Grand Prix Racecourse, Watkins Glen, NY, on 28 July 1973: https://archive.org/details/gd1973-07-28.aud.weiner.106793.flac24; video: https://www.youtube.com/watch?v=6nmo3NKLB7s

Winterland Arena, San Francisco, on 11 November 1973: https://archive.org/details/gd73-11-09.sbd.kaplan.2657.sbefail.shnf

Pauley Pavilion - University of California, Los Angeles, on 17 November 1973: https://archive.org/details/gd73-11-17.sbd.gardner.4749.sbeok.shnf

Denver Coliseum, Denver, on 20 November 1973: https://archive.org/details/gd73-11-20.wolfson.warner.22879.sbeok.shnf

Public Hall in Cleveland, Ohio, on 6 December 1973: https://archive.org/details/gd73-12-06.sbd.kaplan-fink-hamilton.4452.sbeok.shnf

Gizah Sound and Light Theater on 16 September 1978: https://archive.org/details/gd1978-09-16.gems.BEAR.108845.flac24

Winterland Arena, San Francisco (closing of Winterland Arena), on 31 December 1978: https://archive.org/details/gd1978-12-31.fob.akgd224e.holwein.motb-0130.106102.flac16

Giants Stadium, New York, on 10 July 1989: https://archive.org/details/gd89-07-10.sbd.16071.sbeok.shnf

Soldier Field, Chicago, on 9 July 1995: https://archive.org/details/gd95-07-09.sbd.7233.sbeok.shnf

BIBLIOGRAPHY

Alquati, R. *Lavoro e attività* (Rome: Manifestolibri, 1997).

Anitori, R. *Vite insieme. Dalle comuni agli ecovillaggi* (Rome: DeriveApprodi, 2012).

Austin, J. L. *How to Do Things with Words: Second Edition (The William James Lectures)* (Cambridge, MA: Harvard University Press, 1975).

Azais, C., A. Corsani and P. Dieuaide (eds). *Vers un capitalisme cognitif* (Paris: L'Harmattan, 2001).

Baldwin, S. and B. Lessard. *Netslaves* (New York: McGraw Hill, 1999).

Barbrook, R. and A. Cameron. 'The Californian Ideology', in *Science as Culture* 6, no. 1 (1996): 44–72. Available online: http://www.imaginaryfutures.net/2007/04/17/the-californian-ideology-2.

Barlow, J. P. 'A Declaration of the Independence of Cyberspace'. Davos, Switzerland, 8 February 1996. Available online: https://www.eff.org/cyberspace-independence.

Basset, C., P. Grushkin and J. Grushkin (eds), *The Official Book of Deadheads* (New York: Headlands Press, 1983).

Bazzigaluppo, L. *Il governo delle vite. Biopolitica ed economia* (Rome-Bari: La Terza, 2006).

Becattini, *Distretti industriali e sviluppo locale* (Turin: Bollati Boringhieri, 2000).

Bertin, G. *Multinationales et propriété industrielle: le contrôle de la tecnologie mondiale* (Parigi: Presse Universitaire du France, 1985).

Bey, H. (P. L. Wilson), *T.A.Z.: The Temporary Autonomous Zone* (New York: Autonomedia, 1991).

Bin-Italy (ed.), *Un reddito garantito ci vuole. Ma quale? Strumento di libertà o gestione della povertà?*, no. 3, April 2016. Available online: http://www.bin-italia.org/wp-content/uploads/2016/04/QR3_impaginato_Layout-1-3.pdf.

Black, L. and H. Todd. *The Microtrading Revolution: An Insiders Guide to SOES/ECN Trading*, 1st edn (New York: Microtrade Inc., 1998).

Bologna, S. 'The Theory and History of the Mass Worker in Italy', *Common Sense* 11/12 (1987). Available online: https://libcom.org/article/theory-and-history-mass-worker-italy-sergio-bologna.

Bologna, S. and A. Fumagalli (eds), *I lavoratori autonomi di II generazione. Scenari del postfordismo in Italia* (Milan: Feltrinelli, 1997).

Bologna, S., G. P. Rawick, M. Gobbini, A. Negri, L. Ferrari Bravo and F. Gambino, *Operai e Stato* (Milan: Feltrinelli, 1972).

Bonazzi, G. *Il tubo di cristallo. Modello giapponese e fabbrica integrata alla Fiat* (Bologna: Il Mulino, 1993).

Braga, E. and A. Fumagalli (eds). *La moneta del comune. La sfida dell'istituzioone finanziaria del comune* (Rome: DeriveApprodi – Alfabeta, 2015).

Brand, S. *The Last Whole Earth Catalog* (New York: Random House, 1972).

Brooks, D. *Bobos in Paradise: The New Upper Class and How They Got There* (New York: Simon & Schuster, 2004).

Brusco, S. *Piccole imprese e distretti industriali* (Torino: Rosenberg & Seller, 1989).

Caronia, A. *Il cyborg. Saggio sull'uomo artificiale* (Milan: ShaKe Edizioni, 2008).

Cavalli, A. and A. Martinelli (eds). *Gli studenti americani dopo Berkeley* (Turin: Einaudi, 1969).

Chamberlain, A. F. 'Wisdom of the North American Indian-in-Speech and Legend', *American Antiquarian Society* (April 1913).

Chicchi, F. 'Bioeconomia: ambienti e forme della mercificazione el vivente', in A. Amendola, L. Bazzigalupo, F. Chicchi and A. Tucci (eds), *Biopolitica, bioeconomia e processi di soggettivazione* (Macerata: Quodlibet, 2008), 143–58.

Chicchi, F., E. Leonardi and S. Lucarelli. *Logiche dello sfruttamento. Oltre la dissoluzione del rapporto salariale* (Verona: Ombre Corte, 2016).

Churchill, W. and J. V. Watt (eds). *Agents of Repression. The FBI's Secret War Against the Black Panther Party and the American Indian Movement* (Boston: South End Press, 1988).

Clarke, J. 'Grateful Dead's Jerry Garcia: The "Steve Jobs of Rock and Roll"?'. *Forbes*, 30 April 2012. Available online: http://www.forbes.com/sites/joh nclarke/2012/04/30/grateful-deads-jerry-garcia-the-steve-jobs-of-rock-an d-roll/.

Clastres, P. *L'anarchia selvaggia. Le società senza stato, senza fede, senza legge, senza re* (Milan: Eleuthera, 2013).

Codeluppi, V. *Il biocapitalismo. Verso lo sfruttamento integrale di corpi, cervelli ed emozioni* (Turin: Bollati Boringhieri, 2008).

Cohen, R. and R. E. Zelnik. *The Free Speech Movement: Reflections on Berkeley in the 1960s* (University of California Press, 2002).

Cominu, S. 'Cognitive Labour and Industrialization', *Sudcomune*, no. 0 (2015): 30–41.

Coriat, B. *Penser à l'invers* (Paris: C. Bourgois, 1991).

Cowell, M. and K. Hyne. 'Scientific Examination of the Lydian Precious Metal Coinages', in A. Ramage and P. Craddock (eds), *King Croesus' Gold: Excavations at Sardis and the History of Gold Refining* (Cambridge, MA: Harvard University Press, 2000), 169–74.

Davenport, T. *Big Data at Work: Dispelling the Myths, Uncovering the Opportunities* (Boston: Harward Business Review Press, 2013).

De Angelis, M. *Omnia Sunt Communia. On the Commons and the Transformation to Postcapitalism* (London: Bloomsbury, 2017).

De Bagato, P. 'Comun(e)ismo. Lettera a Michele quarantun anni dopo', in C. Morini and P. Vignola (eds), *Piccola enciclopedia precaria* (Milan: Agenzia X, 2015), 229–32.

De Collibus, F. M. and R. Mauro. *Hacking Finance* (Milan: Agenzia X, 2016).

Deleuze, G. 'L'autre journal', no. 1, May 1990, now in G. Deleuze, *Pourparlers (1972–1990)* (Paris: Minuit, 1990), 240–7. Available online: http://www.ecn.org/filiarmonici/Deleuze.html.

Deleuze, G. 'Postscritto sulle società di controllo', in G. Deleuze, *Pourparlers* (Macerata: Quodlibet, 2000).

De Simone, D. and M. Giustini. 'FAZ. Financial Autonomous Zone', in E. Braga and A. Fumagalli (eds), *La moneta del comune. La sfida dell'istituzione finanziaria del commune* (Rome: DeriveApprodi – Alfabeta, 2015), 99–112.

Di Corinto, A. and T. Tozzi. *Hacktivism. La libertà nelle maglie della rete* (Rome: Manifestolibri, 2002).

Doctorow, C. *Down and Out in the Magic Kingdom* (New York: Tor Books, 2003).

Doggett, P. *There's A Riot Going On. Rock Stars, and the Rise and Fall of 60s Counter-culture* (Edinburgh: Canongate Books, 2008).

Draper, H. *Berkeley: The New Student Revolt* (Chicago: Haymarket Books, 2020).

Dyson, E. *Release 2.0: A Design for Living in the Digital Age* (New York: Broadway Books, 1977).

Erodoto. *Storie*, Vol. I (Milan: Mondadori, 2000), fr. 94.

Evelyn, N. 'Our Towns; Ithaca Hours: Pocket Money for Everyman', *New York Times*, 21 January 1996.

Ferrara, P. 'Rethinking Money: The Rise of Hayek's Private Competing Currencies', May 2013. Available online: http://www.forbes.com/sites/peter ferrara/2013/03/01/rethinking-money-the-rise-of-hayeks-private-compet ing-currencies/.

Florida, R. *The Rise of the Creative Class: And How It's Transforming Work, Leisure, Community and Everyday Life* (New York: Basic Books, 2002)

Florida, R. *Cities and the Creative Class* (New York: Routledge, 2005).

Formenti, C. *Incantati dalla rete* (Milan: Raffaello Cortina Editore, 2000).

Formenti, C. *Felici e sfruttati. Capitalismo digitale ed eclissi del lavoro* (Milan: Egea, 2011).

Formenti, C. *Utopie letali. Contro l'ideologia post-moderna* (Milan: Jaca Book, 2013).

Francescato, D. and G. Francescato. *Famiglie aperte: la comune* (Milan: Feltrinelli, 1975).

Fraysse, O. 'How the US Counterculture Redefined Work for the Age of the Internet', in O. Fraysse and M. O'Neil (eds), *Digital Labour and Prosumer Capitalism: The U.S. Matrix* (London: Palgrave Macmillan, 2015), 30–50.

Fuiano, L. *L'emergere della 'nuova' classe creativa*, 2006. Available online: www. Politicaonline.it/?p=368.

Fumagalli, A. 'Lavoro e piccola impresa nell'accumulazione flessibile in Italia. Parte I e Parte II', *Altreragioni* (1996–7): 5, 6.

Fumagalli, A. 'Conoscenza e bioeconomia', *Filosofia e Questioni Pubbliche* IX, no. 1 (October 2004): 141–61.

Fumagalli A. *Bioeconomia e capitalismo cognitivo* (Rome: Carocci, 2007).

Fumagalli, A. 'Le trasformazioni del lavoro autonomo tra crisi e precarietà: il lavoro autonomo di III generazione', *Quaderni di ricerca sull'artigianato* 2 (2015): 228–56.

Fumagalli, A. 'The Concept of Subsumption of Labour to Capital. Towards the Life Subsumption in Bio-cognitive Capitalism', in E. Fisher and C. Fuchs (eds), *Reconsidering Value and Labor in the Digital Age* (London: Palgrave Macmillan, 2015), 224–45.

Fumagalli, A. *Economia Politica del Comune, Sfruttamento e sussunzione vitale nel capitalismo biocognitivo* (Rome: DeriveApprodi, 2019).

Fumagalli, A. 'Bio-Cognitive Capitalism', in B. Skeggs, S. R. Farris, A. Toscano and S. Bromberg (eds), *The SAGE Handbook of Marxism*, vol. 3 (2022), chapter 84, 1537–55.

Fumagalli, A. and G. Giannelli. 'Il fenomeno Bitcoin: moneta alternativa o moneta speculativa?', 17 December 2013. Available online: http://effimera. org/il-fenomeno-bitcoin-moneta-alternativa-o-moneta-speculativa-gianl uca-giannelli-e-andrea-fumagalli/.

Fumagalli, A. and S. Mezzadra (eds). *Crisis in the Global Economy. Financial Markets, Social Struggle and New Political Scenarios* (Cambridge, MA: MIT Press, 2010).

Fumagalli, A. and C. Morini. 'Segmentation du travail cognitif et rente salariale', *Multitudes* 32 (2008): 75–84.

Fumagalli, A. and C. Morini. 'Life Put to Work: Towards a Theory of Life-Value', in *Ephemera* 10, no. 3/4 (2011): 234–52.

Fumagalli, A. and C. Morini. 'Cognitive Bio-capitalism, Social-Reproduction and the Precarity Trap: Why Not Basic Income?', *Knowledge Cultures* 1, no. 4 (2013): 106–26.

Fumagalli, A., S. Lucarelli, E. Musolino and G. Rocchi. 'Digital Labour in the Platform Economy', *Sustainability* 10 (2018): article 1757.

Fumagalli, A., A. Giuliani, S. Lucarelli and C. Vercellone. *Cognitive Capitalism, Welfare and Labour: The Commonfare Hypothesis* (London: Routledge, 2019).

Getz, M. and J. R. Dwork (eds). *The Deadheads Taping Compendium, vol. I, 1959–74* (New York: Owl Books, 1998).

Godani, P. *La vita comune. Per una filosofia e una politica oltre l'individuo*, 'Opera viva', 4 July 2016 (operaviva.info/la-vita-comune).

Graeber, D. *Frammenti di antropologia anarchica* (Milan: Elèuthera, 2006).

Graham, W. A. *The Custer Myth: A Source Book of Custerania* (Harrisburg, PA: The Stackpole Co., 1953). Available online: https://www.astonisher. com/archives/museum/sitting_bull_little_big_horn.html.

Grateful Dead Archive: https://archive.org/details/GratefulDead.

Grim, R. *This Is Your Country on Drugs: The Secret History of Getting High in America* (New Jersey: John Wiley & Sons, 2009).

Hall, S. *Critical Dialogues in Cultural Studies*, edited by D. Morley and K.-H. Chen (New York: Routledge, 1996).

Halloway, J. 'Noi siamo la crisi del lavoro astratto', speech at the UniNomade seminar, Bologna, 11–12 March 2006, typescript.

Hardt, M. and A. Negri. *Commonwealth* (Cambridge, MA: Harvard University Press, 2010).

Hayek, F. von. *The Denationalization of Money. The Argument Refined*, new revised edn (London: The Institute of Economic Analysis, 1978 [orig. edn 1976].

Herrera, R. and C. Vercellone. 'Transformations de la division du travail et endogénéisation du progrès technique', *Economie Appliquée* 55, no. 1 (2002): 63–78.

Holmgren, D. *Permaculture: Principles and Pathways Beyond Sustainability* (London: Holmgren Design Services, 2002).

Kelly, K. *Out of Control: The New Biology of Machines* (London: Fourth Estate (HarperCollins), 1995).

Kelly, K. *New Rules for the New Economy: 10 Ways the Network Economy is Changing Everything* (London: Fourth Estate (HarperCollins), 1999).

Keynes, J. M. *The General Theory of Employment, Interest and Money* (London: Macmillan, 1936 [reprinted 2007]).

Kondratiev, N. *The Long Wave Cycle*, translated by G. Daniels. Introduction by J. Snyder (New York: Richardson and Snyder, 1984).

Lazzarato, M., Y. Moulier Boutang, A. Negri and G. Santilli. *Des entreprises pas comme le outres* (Paris: Publisud, 1993).

Lebert, D. and C. Vercellone. 'Il ruolo della conoscenza nella dinamica di lungo periodo del capitalismo: l'ipotesi del capitalismo cognitivo', in C. Vercellone (ed.), *Capitalismo cognitivo* (Rome: Manifestolibri, 2006), 7–28.

Leight, E. 'President Obama Calls the Grateful Dead an "Iconic American Band" in Touching Tribute', *Billboard*, 5 July 2015.

Lévy, P. *Cyberculture* (Minneapolis: University of Minnesota Press, 2001).

Levy, S. *Hackers: Heroes of the Computer Revolution* (New York: Anchor Press/ Doubleday, 1984).

Lietaer, B. and J. Dunne. *Rethinking Money: How New Currencies Turn Scarcity into Prosperity* (San Francisco: Berret-Koeler Publisher, 2013).

Malvinni, D. *Grateful Dead and the Art of Rock Improvisation* (Plymouth: Scarecrow Press, 2013).

Marazzi, C. 'Capitalismo digitale e modello antropogenetico del lavoro. L'ammortamento del corpo macchina', in J. L. Laville, C. Marazzi, M. La Rosa and F. Chicchi (eds), *Reinventare il lavoro* (Rome: Sapere 2000, 2005), 107–26.

Marazzi, C. *Capital and Language. From the New Economy to the War Economy* (Boston, MA: Semiotext(e), MIT Press, 2008).

Marazzi, C. *The Violence of Financial Capitalism* (Cambridge, MA: Semiotext(e), MIT Press, 2011).

Marazzi, C. *Il comunismo del capitale* (Verona: Ombre Corte, 2015).

Markoff, J. *What the Dormouse Said: How the Sixties Counterculture Shaped the Personal Computer Industry* (New York: Penguin Books, 2005).

Marx, K. *Capital: A Critique of Political Economy* (London: Penguin Books, 1976).

Marx, K. 'Critique of Hegel's Philosophy of Right', Introduction (February 1843). Available online: https://www.marxists.org/archive/marx/works/1843/critique-hpr/.

Marx, K. *Critique of the Gotha Programme*, ch. 1, p. 1. Available online: https://www.marxists.org/archive/marx/works/1875/gotha/ch01.htm.

Marx, K. *Economic & Philosophic Manuscripts of 1844*, third manuscript, ch. 'The Power of Money', fr. XLII. Available online: https://www.marxists.org/archive/marx/works/1844/manuscripts/power.htm.

Marx, K. *Grundrisse* (London: Penguin Books, 1973).

Mattioli, V. *Appunti per una discografia accelerazionista*, 13 April 2015. Available online: www.prismomag.com/appunti-per-una-discografia-accel erazionista.

McNally, D. *A Long Strange Trip. The Inside History of Grateful Dead* (New York: Broadway Books, 2002).

Merywether, N. *Shadow Boxing the Apocalypse. An Alternative History of the Grateful Dead* (San Francisco: Grateful Dead Record, 2015).

Morini, C. *Per amore o per forza. Femminilizzazione del lavoro e biopolitiche del corpo* (Verona: Ombre Corte, 2010).

Morini, and C. and P. Vignola (eds). *Piccola Enciclopedia Precaria* (Milan: Agenzia X, 2015).

Moulier-Boutang, Y. *Cognitive Capitalism* (Hoboken, NJ: John Wiley & Sons, 2007).

Negri, A. *Movimenti nell'Impero. Passaggi e paesaggi* (Milan: Raffaelo Cortina Editore, 2006).

Negri, A. *Il comune come modo di produzione*, June 2016. Available online: www.euronomade.info/?p=7331.

Negri, A. 'General Intellect and Social Individual in the Marxian Grundrisse', 2019. Available online: http://www.euronomade.info/?p=12059.

Nelson, R. and S. Winter. *An Evolutionary Theory of Technical Change* (Boston: Belknap Press, 1982).

Nieves, E. 'Our Towns; Ithaca Hours: Pocket Money For Everyman', *New York Times*, 21 January 1996.

Ohno, T. *Toyota Production System: Beyond Large-scale Production* (New York: Productivity Press Inc., 1995).

Orléan, A. *De l'euphorie à la panique: penser la crise financière* (Paris: Cepremap, Editions Rue d'Ulm, 2009).

Palloix, C. *L'economia mondiale e le multinazionali*, 2 vols (Milan: Jaca Book, 1979 and 1982).

Pasquinelli, M. (ed.). *Gli algoritmi del capitale. Accelerazionismo, macchine della conoscenza e autonomia del comune* (Verona: Ombre Corte, 2015).

Pasquinelli, M. 'Italian Operaismo and the Information Machine', *Theory, Culture & Society* 32, no. 3 (2015): 49–68.

Paulré, B. 'De la *New Economy* au capitalisme cognitif', *Multitudes* 2 (2000): 25–42.

Pedemonte, E. *Personal Media. Storia e futuro di un'utopia* (Turin: Bollati Boringhieri, 1998).

Priore, M. and C. Sabel. *The Second Industrial Divide. Possibilities For Prosperity* (New York: Basic Books, 1984).

Rapelli, S. 'European I-Pros: A Study. Professional Contractors Group (PCG)', 2012. Available online: http://rapelli.free.fr/documents/rapelli _pcg_en.pdf.

Revelli, M. 'Economia e modello sociale nel passaggio tra fordismo e toyotismo', in P. Ingrao and R. Rossanda (eds), *Appuntamenti di fine secolo* (Rome: Manifestolibri, 1995), 161–224.

Rifkin, J. *The Third Industrial Revolution* (London: Palgrave Macmillan, 2011).

Robbins, L. *The Nature and Significance of Economic Science*, 2nd edn (London: Macmillan, 1935).

Roio, D., aka Jaromil. 'Bitcoin, the End of the Taboo on Money', 2013. Available online: http://median.newmediacaucus.org/isea2012-machine-wilderness/bitcom-the-end-of-the-taboo-on-money/.

Rorabaugh, W. J. *Berkeley at War: The 1960s* (Oxford: Oxford University Press, 1989).

Rousseau, J. J. *Of The Social Contract and Other Political Writings* (London: Penguin Books, 2012).

Rudd, M. *Underground. My Life with SDS and Weather Underground* (New York: Harper Collins, 2009).

Sachy, M., aka Radium, 'Freecoin: la cripto-blockchain come bene comune', in E. Braga and A. Fumagalli (eds), *La moneta del comune. La sfida dell'istituzione finanziaria del commune* (Rome: DeriveApprodi – Alfabeta, 2015).

Scaruffi, P. *Grateful Dead*, 1990. Available online: http://www.scaruffi.com/ vol2/grateful.html.

Schwab, K. *The Fourth Industrial Revolution* (London: Penguin Books, 2017).

Shirky, C. *Cognitive Surplus: How Technology Makes Consumers into Collaborators* (London: Penguin Putnam Inc., 2011).

Simonetti, W. *Paolo Virno Dell'esodo*. Available online: http://simonettiwalter. wordpress.com/.

Srnicek, N. and A. Williams, 'Manifesto for an Accelerationist Politics', in J. Johnson (ed.), *Dark Trajectories: Politics of the Outside* (Miami: Name, 2013).

Stallman, R. *GNU Manifesto*, 1985. Available online: http://www.gnu.org/gnu/ manifesto.it.html.

Standing, G. *Precariat. The New Dangerous Class* (London: Bloomsbury, 2011).

Sterling, B. *The Hacker Crackdown: Law and Disorder on the Electronic Frontier* (New York: Bantam, 1992).

Sterling, B. (ed.), *Mirrorshades: The Cyperpunk Anthology* (Ipswich: Arbor House, 1986).

Sterling, B. 'Prefazione a *Mirrorshades*', in Sterling (ed.), *Mirrorshades.*

Taylor, D. *It Was Twenty Years Ago Today* (New York: Random House, 1987).

Terranova, T. *Network Culture* (Rome: Manifestolibri, 2006).

Tronti, M. *Workers and Capital* (London: Verso, 2019).

Turner, R. *From Counterculture to Cyberculture* (Chicago: University of Chicago Press, 2006).

Vecchi, B. *La rete dall'utopia al mercato* (Rome: Ecommons, 2015).

Vercellone, C. (ed.). *Sommes-nous sortis du capitalisme industriel?* (Paris: La Dispute, 2003).

Vercellone, C. (ed.). *Capitalismo Cognitivo* (Rome: Manifestolibri, 2006).

Vercellone, C. 'The Crisis of the Law of Value and the Becoming Rent of Profit', in A. Fumagalli and S. Mezzadra (eds), *Crisis in the Global Economy. Financial Markets, Social Struggle and New Political Scenarios* (Cambridge, MA: MIT Press, 2010), 85–118.

Vercellone, C. et al. (2015), 'Managing the Commons in the Knowledge Economy', Report D3.2, D-CENT (Decentralized Citizens ENgagement Technologies), European Project 2015, May 2015, 24. Available online: http://dcentproject.eu/wp-content/uploads/2015/07/D3.2-compl ete-ENG-v2.pdf.

Vico, G. B. *Principj di una Scienza Nuova Intorno alla Natura delle Nazioni …* (Naples: Felice Mosca, in Italian). English version: *The New Science of Giambattista Vico*, translated by T. G. Bergin and M. H. Fisch (London: Cornell University Press, 1984).

Vincent, R. *Party Music: The Inside Story of the Black Panthers' Band and How Black Power Transformed Soul Music* (Chicago: Lawrence Hill Books, 2013).

Virno, P. *Esercizi di esodo* (Verona: Ombre Corte, 2002).

Virno, P. *A Grammar of the Multitude. For an Analysis of Contemporary Forms of Life* (Boston, MA: Semiotext(e), MIT Press, 2004).

Virno, P. 'A Performative Movement', April 2005. Available online: http://repu
    blicart.net/disc/precariat/virno01_it.htm.
Weir, W. *In the Spirit: Conversation with the Spirit of Jerry Garcia*
    (New York: Three River Press, 1999).
Wolfe, T. *The Electric Kool-Aid Acid Test* (New York: Farrar Straus
    Giroux, 1968).
Zelnik, R. E. *The Free Speech Movement: Reflections on Berkeley in the 1960s*
    (University of California Press, 2002).

INDEX

When the page number is followed by 'n', refer to the footnote on the page.

Morini, Cristina xiiin, 67n, 78n,
    137n, 145n
Morrison, Sterling 23n
Mother McCree's Uptown Jug
    Champions 23
Moulier, Boutang Yann 130n
Musolino Elena xiiin

Negri Antonio xiii, xiv, 101n, 121,
    126n, 130n, 142n
Nelson, Richard 74
net-economy xii, 131–2
network economies xii, xiii, 5,
    130–1, 138
New Riders of the Purple Sage 34
Newton, Huey P. 12
Nico 23, 25n
Nieves, Evelyn 110n

Obama 39
Office of Comptroller of the
    Currency 104
Ohno, Toshito 129n
O'Neil, Mathieu 124n
OpenCoin 115
open-source 17, 64, 70, 79, 103–4,
    106, 117, 124
Orléan, André xiiin, 120n, 131n
Owens, Buck 33

Palloix, Christian 130n
Pasquinelli, Matteo 116n
Paulré, Bernard
Pedemonte, Enrico 69n
Pink Floyd vii, 25, 25n, 27, 30, 35,
    60, 87n
politics 43n, 81, 113–14, 136, 141,
    144
Port Huron Declaration 3
Priore, Michel 130n
proprietary individualism 76, 79
psychedelia 25, 29–30, 32n, 33–4, 37
psychedelic music vi, viii, 4, 22, 42n,
    57, 70, 141

Quicksilver Messenger Service vii,
    13, 21, 23n, 25, 37n

Raizene, Mark 15
Rapelli, Stéphane 103n
Ratdog 38
Rawick, George P. 101n
Reed, Lou 23, 24n
Reich, Wilhelm 51
Republican Party 81
Revelli, Marco 129n
Rich, Don 33n
Riesman, David 43
Rifkin, Jeremy 125n
Ripple 115–16, 119
Robbins, Lionel 108n
Robin Hood Asset Management
    Cooperative 116
Rocchi, Giulia xiiin
Roio, aka Jaromil Denis 114n
Rorabaugh, William J. 2n
Rossanda, Rossana 129n
Roszak, Theodore 44
Rudd, Mark 10, 10n
Rullani, Enzo 130n

Sabel, Charles 130n
Sachy, Marco 111, 111n, 121, 122n
San Francisco 4, 8, 8n, 12–13, 13n,
    14n, 16n, 21, 21n, 23, 23n, 24,
    24n, 25–6, 31, 36, 36n, 41–2,
    42n, 57, 59n, 60, 64, 71n, 73,
    116, 119n, 132
Sartre, Jean-Paul 51
Savio, Mario 2, 2n, 4n, 6
Scaruffi, Piero 19n
Schumpeter, Joseph A. 50
Schwab, Klaus xn
SDS (Students for a Democratic
    Society) 3, 9, 45
Seale, Bobby 11–12
Shakespeare, William 65
Shirky, Clay 67n
Silicon Valley 6, 70–2, 116, 132